in
all
on
it,
ce
els
he
centuries. *The Drumshee Rebels* is Book 8 in the
Drumshee Timeline Series.

For Niall Barry, Conor Davoren, David McGrath,
Declan McMahon and Heather McMahon
of Inchovea School

OTHER TITLES BY CORA HARRISON

The Drumshee Rebels

Drumshee Timeline Series
Book 8

Cora Harrison

Illustrated by Aileen Caffrey

WOLFHOUND PRESS
Celebrating 25 *Years*

First published in 1999 by
Wolfhound Press Ltd
68 Mountjoy Square
Dublin 1, Ireland
Tel: (353-1) 874 0354
Fax: (353-1) 872 0207

© 1999 Cora Harrison

The Arts Council
An Chomhairle Ealaíon

Wolfhound Press receives financial assistance from The Arts
Council/An Chomhairle Ealaíon, Dublin, Ireland.

British Library Cataloguing in Publication Data
A catalogue record for this book is available from the British Library.

ISBN 0-86327-746-2

10 9 8 7 6 5 4 3 2

Cover Illustration: Aileen Caffrey
Cover Design: Sally Mills-Westley
Typesetting: Wolfhound Press
Printed in the UK by Cox & Wyman Ltd, Reading, Berks.

Chapter One

Tuesday 28 June 1921

That was the day when Michael Collins came to Drumshee, the little farm on top of a hill near the west coast of Ireland.

It was the first time Bridget had seen him, although she had often heard her father speak of him. He looked like an ordinary sort of man, and it seemed, at first, an ordinary sort of visit. There was nothing to warn her that a terrible time of danger and terror was about to begin for her family at Drumshee.

All Bridget saw was a tall man, even taller than her father, who had arrived before she got up, and was sitting eating his breakfast with her father when she came down the ladder from her little bedroom in the loft of the cottage. Both men were named Michael, but Bridget's father, Mike McMahon, had blazing red hair, and Michael Collins had black hair. After breakfast they strolled around the farm together, talking earnestly, and every time Bridget came near them she was shooed away. Michael Collins was still there when she came back from school; the two of them were still talking in low tones.

As the day went on, Bridget began to get more and more annoyed. She was the only child in the family, and she was used to visitors taking a lot of notice of her. By the end of the day, she was in a blazing temper. And to top it all off, she was sent to bed early, and that really annoyed her — on such a lovely June evening, too!

Peeping out of her little window in the west gable of the house, she saw her mother come out of the door and climb, with difficulty, up the steep slope towards the *cathair*, the ancient fort behind the cottage. That meant she was going across the fields to see Mrs Arkins, their nearest neighbour. Mam must have been sent out, too, thought Bridget. It must be a really important secret that Da has with Michael Collins.

Maggie McMahon had a sour, disapproving look on her face. That must mean that she didn't like this Michael Collins. Mind you, thought Bridget, she's a bit like this all the time now. Having a baby seems to be having an awful effect on her.

Bridget went back to bed and lay very still, trying hard to hear what her father and his visitor were saying. She had heard many a secret this way while her father and mother were talking downstairs, but tonight she could only hear the steady murmur of a voice. Michael Collins seemed to be doing all the talking. He had an odd way of talking, too, which made him harder to understand. He came from Cork, Bridget's father had told her. That was why he sounded so different.

From time to time, Mike McMahon put in a few words, and one of these words made Bridget prick up her ears.

'Danger,' he said, and the word was clear and distinct; but then he dropped his voice again.

Bridget felt eaten up by curiosity. She had to know what they were talking about. Very quietly, she got out of bed and crept across the floor, carefully avoiding the creaky board in the middle, until she reached the chimney-stack. There had once been a little secret room there, just beside the chimney, completely hidden behind a stone wall. It had been discovered when Bridget was a baby. Some stones had fallen when a great wind had shaken the chimney. Now you could go into the little room; it was just big enough for one person, and it was a lovely little place, warm and cosy. Bridget often played there, and she had discovered that it was a great place to listen to people talking by the fire in the kitchen downstairs.

Now she could hear them — her father's soft County Clare accent, and the singsong Cork voice of Michael Collins.

'You see, Mike, if this list of names is found, it will mean jail or worse for these people,' Michael Collins was saying. 'I have to write down the names and how much each man has given, so that accounts can be kept, but this list is dynamite. I used to keep all the lists under the floorboards of my bedroom, but then I had a tip-off that my house in Dublin would be raided. So now I'm giving the list for each county to a man I can trust. Do you know any man around here?'

'You can trust me,' said Mike McMahon steadily.

'I know that, Mike. But this is a dangerous job. I'm looking for a single man, a man without family responsibilities.'

'I'll do it,' insisted Mike. 'I can be sure of myself; I couldn't say as much for anyone else.'

'Well, you'd be my choice above any other man,' admitted Michael Collins.

'That's settled, then,' said Mike firmly.

Bridget was thrilled. Her father had told her so much about the great Michael Collins and how he was one of the top men organising the struggle against Britain — and now this man was entrusting something very important to her father!

How did he know that his house was going to be raided? she wondered. Even as she thought of the question, she heard her father say, 'How did you know you were going to be raided, Mick? Did they send you a letter from Dublin Castle to tell you?'

Michael Collins laughed. 'Nearly as good,' he said. 'You won't believe it, but my own cousin, Nancy O'Brien, is working as a confidential clerk in Dublin Castle. She has the handling of all the secret coded messages. The poor girl spends most of her dinner hour locked in the toilet, making copies of the messages. She hides them in her corset and her knickers, and then delivers them to me after work.'

'And no one knows that she's your cousin?'

'Not a sinner! Sure, I don't know how these people won an empire!'

Bridget was glowing with excitement. What a brave girl, she thought. I wish I could do something like that. She imagined herself making copies of the coded messages and then walking past all the guards at Dublin Castle to deliver the messages to Michael Collins ....

She was so deep in her thoughts that she missed the next thing her father said, but her attention snapped back to reality when Michael Collins spoke.

'I don't want to put you in any danger, though.'

There was that word again: danger. This was no game.

'You're a married man with a family,' went on Michael Collins. 'Have you got a safe place to hold the list? Somewhere no one knows about?'

'I have,' said Mike McMahon. He hesitated, and Michael Collins interrupted him.

'Don't tell me where. It's best if I don't know too much. I know you're a man to be trusted; if you say you have a safe place, that's good enough for me.'

Bridget was disappointed. She wanted to know where the list was going to be kept.

'I'll leave as soon as it's completely dark,' said Michael Collins. 'No one saw me come and no one will see me go. It's dangerous to have anything to do with me. In April, the Black and Tans burned down my brother's farm and threw him in jail, and his eight children were thrown out on the road on a cold night. And it wasn't long after their mother's death, the poor things.'

Bridget shivered, despite the cosy warmth of the little room. She wondered what had happened to those eight children. Perhaps the neighbours had taken them in. She could hear her father putting more turf on the fire, almost as if he, too, felt cold.

'How have things been with you, down here?' asked Michael Collins, after a short pause.

'Did you hear about Jamesy Rynne?' Mike McMahon asked. 'Jamesy Rynne of Ennistymon?'

There was a silence. Then Michael Collins said, 'No,' and his voice was flat, almost as if he didn't want to know, Bridget thought.

'The Black and Tans killed him,' said her father. After a moment, he went on, 'They poured boiling pitch over him and set him on fire. Then they pushed him into his house and set fire to the thatch.'

There was a long silence from downstairs.

Bridget felt sick. How could anyone do a thing like that? Suddenly she didn't want to hear any more. She was about to crawl back to her bed when the thunderous crack of a poker on the hollow flag-stone in front of the fire made her jump.

'By God,' swore Michael Collins, 'they'll pay for that! He was a good man, and with a young family, too. He had a daughter about the same age as yours. Looked a bit like your girl, too — the same red hair and freckles ....'

How would I feel if that had been my father? thought Bridget, feeling an icy sweat start out on her forehead. Michael Collins was saying something about the West Clare Railway, and something about a man called Curtin who was a spy, but Bridget didn't want to hear any more. She got into bed, pulled the bedclothes over her head and stuck her fingers in her ears. I'm not going to think about that ever again, she thought drowsily, as she began to doze off. I'll never remember it again. I hope that Michael Collins is gone before I wake up and that we never see him again.

Bridget drifted off to sleep. She only woke when she heard the click of the latch of the half-door being raised. She heard the two voices again — just a murmur — and then her father's voice, suddenly quite clear: 'Don't worry. I'll go and hide it this very minute. I've got tinder and a candle with me. I'll walk to the gate with you, and then I'll come back and put it away safely.'

Bridget smiled to herself. She thought she knew where her father was going to hide the list.

He should have given it to me to hide, she thought. She knew of an even better, even safer place — a secret place that no one in the world, except herself, would ever know about.

Chapter Two

The next morning, Michael Collins was gone. No one spoke of him. Bridget went happily off to school, determined to enjoy herself and to forget all about Michael Collins and the danger which might follow him.

It was a good day at school, for once. Bridget didn't really like school very much. She found it boring, and she was always getting into trouble for talking and for losing her temper — usually when her neighbour John Joe Arkins teased her about having red hair. He had been doing that since the day she started school, when she was five years old, and now she would be eleven tomorrow and he was still doing it. Every time he teased her, Bridget lost her temper. It was no good her trying to tease him about having black hair, calling him 'Crow'; he just threw back his head and laughed, his dark eyes sparkling with merriment in his brown face.

However, perhaps today was going to be the start of a new Bridget: she hadn't been in trouble even once. So when they came out of the school porch and John Joe started the usual cry of 'Carrots, Carrots,' she just ignored him and walked on, climbing over the stone stile and turning down the road towards her father's farm.

Chapter Two

For a moment, John Joe was disconcerted. Then he tried again.

'There's a fire on the road!' he cried in mock alarm. 'Look, it's moving down towards Drumshee!'

Bridget still took no notice. Her mother was always telling her to ignore John Joe, and it seemed that it might be going to work. She could hear him running after her. She stopped by the entrance to the Big Meadow and looked at him.

For once, John Joe was the one in a temper. His face was red under the black curls, and his brown eyes, usually sparkling with fun, were angry.

'Anyway, your da is just an IRA man,' he sneered. 'And my mam told me to keep away from your place in case the Black and Tans come looking for him.'

Bridget gasped. Without another glance at her, John Joe went on up the lane towards his house.

Bridget stood without moving for a moment. It wasn't the fact that her father was a member of the Irish Republican Army which upset her — although she was worried about Mrs Arkins knowing all about it — but the thought that the Black and Tans might come looking for him made her heart suddenly start a noisy thumping in her chest. She knew what the Black and Tans were like.

They were English, but they weren't real English soldiers. People said they were the scum from the prisons in England. Bridget had heard how they had gone around Ennistymon, a town only seven miles away, in the middle of the night, driving people out of their houses and shooting them. If they could do that to innocent men and women who were just minding their own business and living their own lives, what might they do to a man who was secretly fighting them? She suddenly remembered the story of Jamesy Rynne that her father had told to Michael Collins. I can understand why Mammy is always fighting with Da these days, she thought. She's frightened for him.

All the same, Bridget was proud of her father. She loved him very much and she wouldn't have changed him for the world. She loved Ireland, too. She knew all the stories about Ireland, and she was the best at history in Inchovea School — not because of the teacher, but because of all the stories her father had told her. He had explained to her why England owned Ireland. He had told her that his own father, Martin, had lived though the Famine more than sixty years before, when millions of people had died while all the corn was shipped out of Ireland to be taken to England. Bridget knew why her father wanted to fight for Ireland, and she was proud of him; but from this moment on, she thought, I'll always be worried about him.

She turned in at the gates of Drumshee and slowly and thoughtfully began the steep climb up the avenue towards her house. When she came to the bend halfway up the avenue, she could see her father in the Togher Field, going towards the *cathair* on the hill behind the little whitewashed cottage. The fort was circular, surrounded by a high stone wall with blackthorn bushes inside it and a deep ditch all the way around the outside. It had a big entrance on the eastern side, and a small gap in the wall on the south-western side. It was the most sheltered and hidden place on the farm.

The *cathair* held a secret, too — an ancient secret. In the middle of the fort was a flagstone, and under that flagstone was a flight of stone steps which led to an underground room. Bridget's father had told her that it had probably been built thousands of years before, by the Iron Age people. This underground room was called a souterrain, and its existence had always been kept a secret by the McMahons. Bridget had never told anyone about the souterrain, not even John Joe.

When Bridget came into the fort that afternoon, her father was standing at the entrance to the souterrain, looking around to make sure that no one else was there, as he always did before he lifted the flagstone. Bridget dumped her school-bag on the wall and ran over to him.

'May I come down too, Da?' she pleaded. Has he hidden the secret list there? she wondered.

'Not now, pet,' said her father, giving her red curls an affectionate rub. Bridget's heart swelled. She loved him so much that she thought she couldn't live if anything happened to him. Perhaps if the Black and Tans got him they would put him in prison or shoot him .... I should tell him what John Joe said, she thought; but she didn't know how to begin.

'Da,' she said, but Mike shook his head.

'No, Bridget, not today — and that's final.' Then he added, teasingly, 'The birthday girl must have a surprise tomorrow.'

'Oh, Da!' Bridget's spirits immediately lifted. It must be a big present that she was going to get tomorrow, something too big to be hidden in the press in her parents' room. She could hardly wait. Without any more arguing, she gave her father a kiss, picked up her bag and went back to the cottage.

Her mother kissed her and put a cup of cold,

creamy buttermilk and a slice of soda bread on the table. 'Where's John Joe?' she asked.

'We had an argument,' said Bridget briefly.

Her mother smiled. 'What about?' she asked.

'Oh, just because he's stupid,' muttered Bridget. 'He doesn't understand anything.'

At that very moment, John Joe was standing in his own kitchen, saying to his mother, 'Mam, I don't understand why Bridget's da is in the IRA. Why does he do it?'

'Goodness only knows,' said Mrs Arkins. 'He minds everyone's business but his own. Spends too much time reading and thinking about things, like all the McMahons. They were a bit wild, too, all those boys. I remember Patrick, the eldest one — he was a holy terror. He'd dare anything.'

'Yes, but Mam,' said John Joe impatiently, not wanting to be sidetracked into stories about the past, 'what is the IRA for? I don't understand.'

'Well,' said his mother, draining the water from the potatoes, 'you see, the IRA used to be a sort of secret army, but now they've taken over a lot of the country and they want to set Ireland free from being ruled by England. The English don't want to let Ireland go, so they've sent over the Black and Tans. They're called that because of the uniforms — they wear tan-coloured trousers and black jackets. You've seen them around, haven't you — down in Ennistymon, driving around in those lorries? The Black and Tans are trying to frighten people off from joining the IRA, so if they hear of anyone having anything to do with it, they burn the house over his head.'

'It doesn't seem fair, does it?' said John Joe, beginning to feel some sympathy for Mike McMahon.

'Ah, John Joe,' said his mother, shaking her head, 'life is never fair, especially for poor people. This fighting has gone on for hundreds of years, and it hasn't done any good. Look at the poor people in 1798 — thousands of them tortured and killed, and no one any better off at the end of it. And then there was Cromwell, a hundred and fifty years before that, even. People tried to fight against him too, but nothing came of that, either. It's best for poor people like ourselves to keep our heads down and not cause any trouble. Anyway, don't keep me talking while I should be doing the dinner. Go and tell your father and the rest of them that it will be ready in five minutes.'

As John Joe was going out, his mother said, 'I'll tell you one thing, John Joe: Mike McMahon will bitterly regret the day that he got himself mixed up with that gang. And as for that poor wife of his, Maggie — well, I'm sorry for her. One of these days you'll see the Black and Tans' lorry going up that avenue to Drumshee, and that will mean prison, or worse, for Mike McMahon.'

Chapter Three

As soon as Bridget woke up, she knew that her birthday was going to be a lovely sunny day. She got out of bed and went to the window. Her little loft bedroom, snug under the thatch, had its window on the west side, so she couldn't see the sun, but she could see the shadows of the trees, and already she could smell the heat in the air. The cock was crowing loudly, and as she stuck her head further out of the window she saw the Muscovy ducks, their black and white and silver flashing in the sunlight, fly past on their way to the river. Da must be up, thought Bridget; all the poultry are out of their houses already.

She closed the window and dressed herself in her school frock, pulling on the white pinafore which she wore to keep her frock clean, and buttoned her brown leather boots. The next day, the holidays would begin, and then she would be allowed to go barefoot and wear her cotton dress, not this scratchy serge.

Humming a little tune, Bridget climbed down the ladder into the kitchen. Her mother was already there, bending over the fire and making tea from the heavy blackened kettle which swung on the iron crane.

'Happy birthday, Bridget,' she said wearily, straightening herself with her hand on her back. All her life, Bridget had thought that her mother was the most beautiful woman in the world. Maggie McMahon was tall and dark and very slim, and when she went to mass on Sundays, wearing the antique gold necklace which had been in the McMahon family for generations — it was supposed to be hundreds, or even thousands, of years old — she looked like a grand lady. But no one could call her beautiful now, and she certainly wasn't slim. After eleven years without childbearing, Maggie was expecting a baby in August.

'How's your back, Mam?' said Bridget, trying to be sympathetic. Secretly she felt impatient. She hoped that when the baby was born Maggie would change back to the familiar mother, kind, patient and fun-loving, and that this bloated, nagging stranger would disappear.

'Not so good,' said her mother, with her usual exhausted air. 'I got hardly any sleep last night. Still,' she added, with an effort to be cheerful, 'don't worry about me now. Sit down and have your breakfast. I've cooked an egg for you. No, don't sit there, you'll have the sun in your eyes. Sit on the other side of the table, with your back to the door.'

Bridget sat down, feeling rather puzzled. The two halves of the door were open, it was true, but the early-morning sun wasn't that bright. Still, her father had asked her not to argue with her mother until the baby was born, so she obediently sat down in the unfamiliar place.

She had just finished her egg when she saw her mother's eyes look over her head, towards the door. She half-turned; then a large, hard hand covered her eyes and her left hand was placed on something cold and shiny and smooth. There was a faint smell of rubber in the air. Bridget moved her hand and felt a triangular shape — not metal; it must be leather — and then, further down, something hard and curved.

'It's a bicycle!' she shouted, jumping up from the table.

Her father laughed and took his hand away from her eyes. It was, indeed, a beautiful bicycle, full-sized, with a neat basket in front. Bridget had never dreamt of getting such a marvellous present. Bicycles cost so much money that very few children owned them. She would be the only scholar at Inchovea School to have one.

'May I ride it to school?' she asked eagerly.

Her father laughed, and even her mother smiled.

'I don't think it would be worth it,' said Mike. 'It's only about two hundred yards to the school. But I'll tell you what you can do. Tomorrow is the first day of the summer holidays, and you and John Joe can go off for the day. I'm sure his father will lend him his bike. I often see John Joe on it.'

Bridget scowled. 'I'm not speaking to John Joe these days,' she said.

Her father raised his eyebrows and gave a half-smile. 'See how you feel at the end of the day,' he advised. 'It's never worth quarrelling with your neighbours, you know. We all need our neighbours.'

Bridget said nothing. She didn't want to tell her father what John Joe had said. In fact, she didn't even want to think about it. And when, half an hour later, she found John Joe waiting at the gate, she just walked past him.

John Joe ran after her. 'I'm sorry I teased you, Bridget,' he said. 'This is for you. Happy birthday.'

He pressed a small bag into her hand, and Bridget couldn't keep herself from opening it. Inside were some bull's-eye sweets, her favourites. She couldn't resist taking one. After all, Da is probably right, she thought; we should be on good terms with our neighbours. Without saying a word, she held out the bag to John Joe. He took a sweet too, and they sucked them happily and went down the road together as if they had never quarrelled.

'Guess what,' said Bridget, in between sucks of the sweet. 'I've got a bicycle for my birthday, and I'm allowed to go off for the day on it tomorrow. If you can come with me, we'll bring a picnic and go down to Ennistymon. Do you think your da will let you borrow his bike?'

'Sure to,' said John Joe, who as the youngest of ten had his father and mother firmly wrapped around his little finger. 'Let's get up really early, about six in the morning. Then we can cycle while it's nice and cool, and we'll sit by the river in Ennistymon and have a good rest before we come back.'

The last day of term was always fun. No one did very much work; they were all busy tidying away the maps, washing out the inkwells and stacking the desks so that the school could be cleaned during the holidays. Everything went well for Bridget: no one called her names, the master didn't care how much talking she did today, everyone was excited to hear about the bicycle, and she and John Joe were friends again.

Things got even better when Bridget got home that evening. Her mother had baked a lovely cake with currants and raisins in it, especially for her birthday. Maggie's good mood lasted right up to Bridget's bedtime. She packed a special lunch for Bridget to take on the picnic the next day and put a bottle of buttermilk in the shady, fern-fringed well to keep cool overnight.

'You can go as early as you like,' she told Bridget. 'If you really do want to go at six o'clock, you don't need to wake us. Just have some breakfast and then be off — that is, if you do wake up as early as that. I won't be too surprised if I have to drag you out of bed at nine o'clock, as usual.'

'You won't,' said Bridget with determination. 'I'm going to be up at dawn.'

That night, before going to sleep, Bridget banged her head six times on the pillow. The girls in school swore that always worked. So when Bridget woke up, some time later, she was sure it was six o'clock.

She looked out of the window. It certainly looked bright outside, though it was a strange, white brightness. She felt fresh and excited at the thought of the day's holiday ahead of her. She got out of bed and dressed quietly, although her parents' bedroom was on the east side of the house and she had little fear of waking them until she actually started to go down the ladder, carrying her shoes in her hand. She reached the bottom of the ladder without a single creak.

Then she stopped in astonishment. The clock's hands were big and black, and the kitchen was full of light, so there could be no mistake: it was only twelve o'clock. Who would have thought that it could be so bright at midnight?

Bridget opened the door and stole out into the farmyard. The shadows of the hedges were etched black and sharp on the silvery green of the grass; in the distance a cow coughed. Then she heard another sound. It was a voice, speaking low, but it carried clearly in the silence of the night. It came from behind the house, from the old *cathair*.

Bridget slipped on her shoes and started to climb up towards the fort. Moving as quietly as a fox, she reached the ash tree beside the fort without making a sound. This ash was a huge old tree; its branches touched the ground, forming a little cave. There was a shrine there which held a little ancient statue of Saint Brigid, and underneath the statue was a secret place which only Bridget knew about.

On her hands and knees, she crawled across the cave. Carefully she parted the branches beyond the little shrine and peeped over the wall. What she saw filled her with astonishment and excitement.

There were men in the fort. Some of them were strangers, but some were neighbours, well known to Bridget. Her father was in the middle, and his arms were full of guns. While Bridget watched, he handed the guns out, one to each waiting man. Then they lined up and began a drill. Up and down they marched, presenting arms and pretending to fire. Filled with excitement, Bridget watched.

After about half an hour, the men began to file out of the fort, down the Togher Field and along the little laneway which led to the road. Bridget waited for a minute and then followed them, taking care to keep hidden in the shadow of the hedge.

When the men reached the road, they turned and marched along the road towards Wilbrook. When they reached the bridge over the River Fergus, Bridget stopped. She wondered whether she should keep following them, just to see where they were going, but she decided not to. Her mother might wake and find that she was gone, and then there would be trouble. She might not be allowed to have

her day out with John Joe. She must not risk that.

She turned to go back; and then her eye was caught by a movement in a big ash tree at the top of the hill. In the bright moonlight, she could see the dark, moving shape clearly. It was a man; she could see the back of his head, his juglike ears and his black hair sticking up in tufts. He had his back turned to her; he was watching the men marching up the road to Wilbrook.

I suppose he's the lookout man, thought Bridget. I'd better get back before he sees me.

Very quietly and cautiously, Bridget withdrew. All the way home, her mind was working busily. The guns must have been hidden in the souterrain, she thought. That was why Da didn't want me to go down there.

Funnily enough, she was no longer worried about her father. She was filled with a great pride in him. All her life, for as long as she could remember, he had been telling her stories about Ireland, and she had become as great a patriot as he was. She wished that she too could fight for Ireland. Her father had told her about the boys in Dublin, none of them much older than she was, who carried messages and acted as lookouts for the IRA. Because they just looked like ordinary children around the streets, the Black and Tans took no notice of them, and they had saved many soldiers' lives. They were called the Fianna, the warriors. Her father was a soldier; if only she could join the Fianna and help him and Michael Collins in their struggle to free Ireland!

Bridget got into bed, but just before she fell asleep, she remembered the man in the tree. Was he really the lookout man — really part of the IRA?

Or could he be a spy?

Chapter Four

After her midnight adventure, Bridget did sleep in, but fortunately only until seven o'clock; and when she wheeled her bike down the steep hill of the avenue, she found that John Joe had only just arrived. Luckily she saw him coming, and he saw her coming, so neither could tease the other about oversleeping.

The first mile was great fun. It was downhill all the way to the crossroads and they free-wheeled down, startling the swallows who swooped across the little road, busy with their unending task of catching insects to feed their hungry nestlings. After the crossroads, where they turned left to go into Ennistymon by the Ballagh road, it was harder work, as the road began to climb steadily. John Joe was more used to cycling than Bridget; Mr Arkins was a small man and his bicycle was the right size for long-legged John Joe, who, in fact, rode it more than his father did. But although Bridget had occasionally borrowed her father's bicycle, it was far too big for her, so she hadn't had much practice. Still, she was determined not to give in, so she struggled on gamely until they reached Lickeen Lake. To her relief, John Joe proposed that they have a rest there. So by the time they reached Ennistymon, it was nearly lunch-time.

Ennistymon was a very fine town, they both thought. It was full of shops selling anything you could ever want. Bridget and John Joe wandered around the streets and bought some sweets and two small cakes with Bridget's birthday money. Then they wheeled their bicycles down a little lane towards the river, to eat their lunch.

They were hot and tired, and the river looked lovely and cool, sparkling in the sun. They came to the Cascades, where the river fell from a height down a series of flat rocks. Clouds of spray rose up from the waterfall.

John Joe looked at Bridget with mischief in his eyes.

'I dare you to walk across the rocks, right under the water,' he challenged.

Bridget hesitated for a moment and looked at her cotton dress. It was her favourite dress. It had been made for her by her cousin Kitty, who was a dressmaker in America. It fitted her beautifully, and it was a lovely shade of bright green which went well with her red hair.

Still, it was a very hot day, and the dress would soon dry. Without any more hesitation, Bridget took off her shoes and stockings and went carefully across the wet, slimy rocks, sliding her feet in front of her and balancing herself with her arms. At first the water on her sun-heated skin was like a sharp pain, it was so cold; but she soon got used to it, and it felt so deliciously cool that she thought she could stay there for ever.

'Come on in, it's lovely!' she shouted. When she saw John Joe hesitating, she chanted, 'Scaredy-cat, scaredy-cat!'

In an instant, John Joe was beside her. They

danced up and down under the cool, foaming water, running in and out under it just for the fun of feeling the icy shock of the weight of falling water on their hot heads.

However, after about half an hour of this, their fun was spoilt by the chemist from the Medical Hall seeing them from his back window and coming out of the shop and threatening to tell their mothers. Bridget stuck her tongue out at him, behind his back, but they didn't dare to go on playing there. So, streaming water, John Joe's hair plastered to his head like a smooth cap and Bridget's hair in tight corkscrew curls, they wheeled their bikes along the path beside the river until they were out of the chemist's sight. There was a clump of trees behind the police barracks, and they ate their lunch there. By now they were really hungry, and they finished every last crumb in both of their baskets. Then they lay side by side, dreamily looking at the river.

'Let's play a game,' said Bridget, feeling that if they didn't do something soon they would fall asleep and waste their day of freedom.

'What shall we play, then?' asked John Joe, yawning widely.

'I know,' said Bridget. 'Let's play spies. We've been given an important message to deliver to the IRA, and we have to creep though the wood and not make a single sound or we'll be caught and hanged.'

They played this game for about half an hour, but in the end John Joe got bored. It would have been a better game, he thought, if they'd had some other children to be the Black and Tans who were hunting them; but neither he nor Bridget was willing to be the Black and Tans. So he got another idea.

'I know,' he said. 'We'll pretend that the IRA have commissioned us to blow up the Ennistymon barracks. They've given us some gunpowder, and we have to sneak up through the back garden and throw it in that open window, there.'

'Children don't do things like blowing up places,' objected Bridget. 'Even the Fianna just carry messages.'

'Oh, don't worry about that,' said John Joe impatiently. 'This will be much more fun. Look, give me the empty sweet bag. We'll fill it with this powdery dirt. That can be the explosive.'

And, indeed, Bridget had to admit that it was much more fun. To begin with, it was certainly more dangerous, and that added a great spice of excitement. It was well known that the Black and Tans were capable of firing on children; they had done it many times. They both knew that, even if they weren't shot, they would be in deep trouble if they were caught. So it was with a great thrill of excitement that they squeezed through the broken fence at the bottom of the barracks garden.

Luckily, the garden was quite neglected, and the grass was as tall as a five-year-old child. Bridget and John Joe lay flat on their stomachs and, inch by inch, wriggled forward. It was horribly uncomfortable. The pollen from the grass and the dust from the dry earth got into Bridget's nose, and she had to struggle for a few minutes to hold back a sneeze.

It seemed ages before they saw the rough blocks of limestone ahead of them and knew that they had reached the wall. Very cautiously, they straightened up. The barracks had been built on sloping ground, so the tops of their heads just barely reached the windowsill.

Chapter Four

John Joe was just about to throw the bag of dry earth in through the window when the sound of a voice inside made them suddenly freeze with terror. Funnily enough, it wasn't an English voice they heard — although it was speaking English — but a voice with a local accent.

'I'm telling you, sir,' said the voice, with an un- pleasant crawling sound to it which made Bridget squirm, 'I'm telling you the truth. I saw the ten of them on the road to Wilbrook, in the middle of the night, and every man of them carrying a gun. I'm telling you, they're planning to blow up the West Clare Railway, near Wilbrook, and they'll be doing it to- morrow — I heard them say they'd do it on Saturday. And all ten of them will be there. Now isn't that worth a pound to you? I'm a poor man, you know. I worked for the RIC in Tipperary, but when the IRA got to know about me I had to leave in a hurry, with- out a penny to my name. And if they get wise to me here, it's my body you'll be finding on the West Clare Railway line.'

Very cautiously, Bridget stood on her toes and raised her head until her nose was level with the windowsill. Now she could see into the room. She couldn't see the policemen — they must have been sitting down — but she did see the back of the head of the man who was speaking: a man with black hair, sticking up in tufts, and jug-handle ears.

It was the man who had been in the tree the night before.

Bridget didn't make a sound, and she didn't turn to go back the way they had come. She slid silently along the side of the barracks, keeping close to the wall until she reached the corner. Then she climbed the fence and set off, running as fast as she could, down the lane to where they had left their bicycles.

John Joe followed her, puzzled and slightly scared. Bridget picked up her bicycle and pushed it along the river path until they came to another lane; then, getting on her bicycle, she began to pedal as fast as she could, up the steep road that led to Ballagh.

'What's the matter?' said John Joe, after they had gone about a mile.

'Nothing,' said Bridget tersely.

'Do you think your father might be in on it — in on that IRA business?'

'Shut up!' said Bridget furiously. 'Shut up, shut up! Don't you ever dare say anything about my father and the IRA!'

'All right, then. I'm going home. And don't you ever speak to me again, you bad-tempered carrot-head!'

With that, John Joe speeded up and moved well ahead of Bridget. She was glad to be rid of him, but she still cycled as quickly as she could. Now she knew the meaning of the scene she had watched the night before. After she had gone back to bed, the men, carrying their guns, must have gone up the hill towards Wilbrook, where they must have been seen and overheard by that spy who had been in the barracks.

Suddenly she thought of the last words she had heard Michael Collins say. What was it he had said? Something about the West Clare Railway?

Bridget shook her head impatiently. It didn't really matter. Only one question mattered now.

Would she be in time to warn her father?

She was hot and tired by the time she reached Drumshee, and her heart sank when she came to the top of the avenue and saw her Uncle Tom, her mother's brother, coming out of the cow cabin carrying two buckets of milk. Her father must be away from home and not expected back. There was no other reason for Tom to be doing the milking.

All that evening, Bridget was silent. She didn't once ask where her father was; she knew she would only be told lies. She thought that her Uncle Tom and her Aunt Mary probably knew, because they both had disapproving looks on their faces. Neither of them liked her father, and Bridget knew that he laughed at them behind their backs and called them a pair of West Britons.

When both of them went out to see to the animals, Bridget decided that this was her only opportunity.

'Mam,' she said, 'do you know where Da is? I heard in Ennistymon that the Black and Tans know there's going to be an attack on the West Clare Railway line. Is Da there?'

A flicker of fear crossed Maggie's face, but she shook her head resolutely. 'I don't know where he is, Bridget,' she said aloud, as her brother and sister-in-law came back into the kitchen. 'You know what your father's like — always out with his friends, not worrying about his wife, no matter how she's feeling. It's all very well to be worrying about your country, but a man should think about his wife and children first, and leave the danger to the young bachelors. He's risking our lives as well, you know.'

Bridget stared at her mother in contempt, then turned and walked out. She climbed the hill behind the house and went into the fort. Looking all around her carefully, as her father had trained her to, she lifted the flagstone and went down into the souterrain.

Except for some jars of oats and a few sacks of potatoes, there was nothing there. Certainly there were no guns.

However, she supposed that her father, if he was carrying a gun, probably wouldn't come home until after dark. Perhaps she would still have a chance to warn him. After all, there was no reason for him to stay out all night. Wilbrook was only about two and a half miles away; he could walk that in three-quarters of an hour.

Bridget had a quick look around to see if Michael Collins's list was hidden anywhere — maybe in one of the jars of oats, she thought — but she couldn't find it. Perhaps her father had taken it with him. She hoped not. That would be even more dangerous.

Chapter Five

Saturday 2 July 1921

When Bridget woke up the next morning, at six o'clock, her head felt heavy and she ached all over. As well as being stiff from the exercise of the day before, she had slept very badly, waking at the slightest noise and then lying awake wondering whether her father had come home yet.

She dressed quietly and went downstairs. The door of her parents' room was open. She peeped in. There was her mother, lying on her back and snoring slightly, her swollen body lifting the bedclothes into a grotesque heap; but beside her the bed was empty. Bridget had to face the facts: her father had definitely not come home.

She poured herself a cup of milk and ate a piece of soda bread. She knew what she had to do, and as far as she could see there was no way out of it. She would have to go up to Wilbrook and try to find her father and his friends before they did anything to the West Clare Railway line.

She found a piece of paper and wrote a note to her mother.

'Gone for a cycle ride. Be back as soon as possible.

Love,

Bridget.'

On her way down the avenue, she let the ducks and

the hens out of their houses and fed the hens. She looked guiltily at the four cows, but she really couldn't spare the time to milk them. After all, she argued with herself, John Joe's mother has had twelve children, and I bet she kept on working all the time when she was pregnant. My mother is making such a fuss about this baby, she thought jealously. You'd think no one ever had a baby before.

She turned her mind away from her guilt by wondering whether she should ask John Joe to come with her. She decided not to. She had been horrible to him yesterday; but the less said about her father and his membership of the IRA, the better. I'll make it up with John Joe later, she decided, as she carefully closed the gate to the avenue. Once she had saved her father's life, there would be time for everything else.

The road to Wilbrook was very steep, even steeper than the road to Ennistymon, and time after time Bridget had to get off her bicycle and walk. However, it wasn't far, and by seven o'clock she had reached the road which linked Corofin and Ennistymon. Everything looked calm and peaceful, and she could see the little railway line curving along the valley in the distance.

The big problem now was to find out where the men were hiding. Bridget guessed that they wouldn't attempt to blow up the line or to take off the rails until shortly before the train was due; if they did, someone might spot the damage and warn the train — which was probably carrying guns, or else reinforcements for the barracks at Ennistymon or at Miltown Malbay.

Bridget didn't really know what to do, so she cycled slowly along the road, looking carefully over the hedges and into the fields. She hoped that, if her father was hiding behind one of the high walls of Roxton House or in a ditch somewhere, perhaps he would see her; but only the singing of the birds broke the silence of the early morning.

She reached Corofin Station without hearing or seeing anything, and turned to go back. The man at the barracks had definitely spoken of Wilbrook, so she had come too far. It would be stupid for the IRA to attack the line at a station, where the stationmaster would see them.

Perhaps they were on the other side of Wilbrook. Bridget cycled back again, still looking and listening. At the crossroads which led down to Inchovea, she caught sight of a faint movement in a clump of trees, across a field from her. She got off her bicycle and stared, but she saw nothing. She decided it must have been her imagination, or the sunlight glinting off the glossy green beech leaves. She got on her bicycle again and cycled slowly along until she reached Wilbrook schoolhouse; then she turned down the road to the station.

At the station she stopped and looked along the track. This part of the West Clare Railway line was very open, and somehow Bridget didn't think any attempt would be made here. The men would be in too much danger of being seen.

Once again she turned her bicycle and cycled back to the crossroads. She would look in that clump of beech trees. She left her bicycle under a hedge and crept across the field, keeping carefully in the shade of the hedge until she reached the copse.

A minute later Bridget thought that her heart would stop with terror. A large rough hand had been placed over her face, and she knew instinctively that this was not her father, nor one of his friends.

She wriggled around and saw the familiar dreaded uniform, the black jacket and the tan-coloured trousers. It was the Black and Tans, a whole group of them. She could see now why she hadn't spotted them earlier: they all had branches, broken from the beech trees, tied to their heads and jackets and piled around them. They lay there silently and watched, with menacingly cold eyes, while Bridget's captor tied a dirty handkerchief around her mouth and used a piece of rope to tie her legs and wrists until she was trussed up like a goose at the market.

A wave of anger came over her as she lay there helplessly. She was furious with them for treating her like that, and she was even more furious with herself. How stupid she had been, to cycle up and down the road like that! They must have guessed what she was doing. It was a good job that her father hadn't come out to her. If he had, the Black and Tans would immediately have seen where the IRA men were hiding. But now she had no hope of rescuing him.

The wind that day was coming from the north-east; so when the little train from Ennis pulled in at Corofin Station, two miles away, the sound of its whistle carried clearly. Bridget froze with terror, and she could almost feel the tension of all the men around her. No one moved, but she knew that they were waiting for a sound.

And then the sound came. It was unmistakable: it was the sound of heavy sledgehammers on the rails, and of iron girders being ripped from the ground.

The Black and Tans, no longer trying to hide, jumped to their feet and ran across the fields. Shots rang out,

a scream of agony, shouts, curses; but Bridget could do nothing. Frantically she wriggled on her stomach to the edge of the clump of beech trees and managed to stand up with her back against a tree-trunk.

She could see everything plainly now. The fight, if there had been a fight, was over. One of the Black and Tans was walking up the track, waving a red flag, and Bridget could hear the noise of the train slowing down. The rest of the Black and Tans had surrounded the IRA men and were dragging them across the field towards Wilbrook Station. Bridget could see the men very clearly, and she recognised them: they were the men whom she had seen on that moonlit night only a few days before.

But there were only nine of them. One man was missing. Her father was not there.

At first, Bridget thought she must be mistaken; but no, she could see everyone. There was no doubt in her mind: her father wasn't there.

Five minutes later, she saw a big military lorry roar up the little road, and she knew that it must have been hidden behind the shed at the station. She waited tensely while it passed the crossroads, but it didn't slow down. Either the Black and Tans had forgotten about her, or they had decided that she wasn't worth bothering about.

She could see the heads of the prisoners sitting in the back of the lorry. There were five dark-haired men, three fair men and one bald-headed man, but there was definitely no man with red hair.

Bridget was intensely puzzled. She was sure that her father was one of the leaders, and it wouldn't be like him not to be first at the scene of danger. Perhaps he had been injured — or even killed — and they had left his body there beside the railway line ....

Again and again, Bridget rubbed her bound hands against the tree-trunk, frantically trying to loosen the knots, but she could do nothing. The rope was tied too securely. She couldn't even shout for help, because the gag was still over her mouth. She looked around desperately, but there was no one to help her. She tried to wriggle further out into the field, but she scraped her knee on a sharp stone, and she was making so little progress, anyway, that it hardly seemed worth it. The road was at least five hundred yards away; she would never get that far.

Her knee was bleeding badly, but she couldn't do anything for it. I hope I don't bleed to death, she thought. What was it Granny used to say, when she was alive? Put a cobweb on it; that will stop the bleeding .... Bridget's mother had never allowed her to try this out, but now she thought she would risk the dirt if only she could find an obliging spider. In any case, even if she didn't bleed to death, she hated the sticky feeling of the blood trickling down her leg.

At the best of times, Bridget couldn't bear to do nothing, and now she was so uncomfortable that every minute seemed endless. Again and again she tried to wriggle her hands free, but her wrists were getting more and more sore with every attempt. She looked at the sky. It must be about ten o'clock by now, she thought; surely the Black and Tans aren't just going to leave me here to starve to death, like an animal in a trap? No, she told herself. They're bound to remember me and come back to untie me.

She kept telling herself that for the next half-hour or so, but then a little cold thought trickled into her head: what about that man in Ennistymon? They set him on fire and burned him to death in his own house. They won't care about you, said the thought in her head. They won't care whether you live or die.

Bridget knew that was true, and for the first time she began to be scared, as well as angry. If only she had had the sense to tell John Joe where she had gone .... If only she hadn't quarrelled with him .... It had been her fault, too, she knew that; he had only been trying to be helpful when he had asked if she was afraid for her father. Still, there was no use crying over spilt milk. She had quarrelled with him, and she had told no one where she was going. So her only hope was to get to one of the cottages on the Wilbrook road and get someone to untie her. At least her knee had stopped bleeding. Perhaps she could take little jumps and cross the field that way.

It was hard work, but Bridget kept going. She didn't take long jumps, in case she fell again; she took little short hops, with rests in between. It seemed like an hour before she reached the middle of the field. She was soaked in sweat and absolutely exhausted. Her legs were trembling violently. I have to sit down, she thought. I have to have a rest. I just can't keep going like this any longer.

She looked around desperately. There was no sign of anyone. The field had recently been cut for hay, and there were no cows in it; there was no reason for the farmer to come there for days.

Bridget was about to sit down in despair when she saw a movement at the Inchovea crossroads. Someone with black hair was moving along the road.

She strained her eyes. Could it be? It was too good to be true!

And at that moment a shout came across the field.

'Bridget, is that you?'

Bridget tried her best to shout back, but with the heavy gag muffling her mouth, the shout was more like a groan. But it didn't matter. John Joe had seen her. In a minute, the neat black head was rising above the wall, and then he was down on the other side and running across the field as fast as he could.

'It's a good job you have such red hair,' he said, as he untied her. 'You showed up really well against the grass. Now, if you had green hair, I would never have seen you.'

Bridget rubbed her numb ankles and wrists and tried to glare at him; but, despite herself, she had to laugh at the thought of what she would look like with green hair. It would be even worse than red hair, she supposed.

'What happened?' asked John Joe. 'I met the postman and he told me he'd seen you cycling up Wilbrook way, so I thought I'd see what you were up to.'

'It was the Black and Tans who tied me up,' Bridget said.

John Joe was silent for a moment. His face had gone white, Bridget saw; but when he spoke, he deliberately kept his voice light.

'You're lucky they didn't shoot you,' he said. 'Or tie you to the railway line just before the train came. I saw a film once where that happened to a girl.' He gave a quick, half-scared glance around and turned slightly pale under his tan.

'Don't worry,' said Bridget. 'They're gone. They went hours ago.'

'I'm not worried,' said John Joe, with an effort. 'But I think we should get out of the way before they remember about you and come back. Anyway, did you find your father? He is in on this business, isn't he?'

'Yes, he is,' said Bridget. 'But I haven't found him. He wasn't with the others. I don't know what happened to him.'

It's no good trying to pretend any longer, she thought. John Joe had heard what that spy had said. He wasn't stupid. She might as well be honest with him.

'I have to go and look at the railway line, John Joe,' she added. 'I saw the Black and Tans take away the men, but my da wasn't with them. He might have been wounded or something. I heard shots.'

John Joe looked at her dubiously, but said nothing. She knew what he was thinking: her father was more likely to be left lying dead than to be left lying wounded. If he had been wounded, the Black and Tans would just have put him in the lorry. However, Bridget resolutely turned her mind away from that possibility. She was determined to rescue her father and to bring him safely back to Drumshee.

'Let's go down towards Wilbrook Station,' she said hurriedly.

There was no one at Wilbrook Station. Bridget and John Joe moved cautiously along the track until they came to the place where the IRA had tried to derail the train. There was nothing to be seen there, either. A couple of pickaxes were lying beside the rails; that was all.

In the distance, they could see a woman in a garden looking at them curiously.

'That's Mrs Meeney, who lives in the crossing cottage,' said John Joe in a low voice. 'She has to close the gates whenever the train crosses the road there at Newtown. Let's cycle up there and ask her if she knows anything.'

Mrs Meeney was only too glad to have a gossip. John Joe only had to say, 'Did you see the Black and Tans' lorries, Mrs Meeney?' for her to launch into the whole story.

'I'm still shaking like a leaf,' she ended. 'Those IRA lads from Ennistymon should leave the railway alone. I've got a nice little job here, minding the crossing, and I can do my bit of gardening while I watch for the train — I don't want the track blown up! Still, I hated to see the boys being taken away by those Black and Tans — murdering blackguards, they are.'

'Did they take all the men with them, or were any of them killed?' asked John Joe, while Bridget clenched her nails into the palms of her hands.

'Oh, no, none of them were killed. One got a bullet in the leg, but that was all. They took them all away in the lorry. There was no one else there, that's certain. They had a good hunt around afterwards, but they'd got them all.'

'Oh, well, we'd better let you get on with your gardening,' said John Joe, with his usual friendly politeness. 'Goodbye, Mrs Meeney.'

'Goodbye, John Joe, and goodbye to your friend, too,' said Mrs Meeney, looking curiously at Bridget. Bridget felt her cheeks flame. Why was Mrs Meeney looking at her like that? Had she seen her father? Bridget knew that she looked like her father; everyone always remarked on that ....

Mrs Meeney, however, only smiled kindly at her. 'You're looking better now,' she said. 'I thought you looked very pale before. Sure, God love you, I could see all the freckles standing out on your face like currants in a bread-mix.'

'How would you like me to knock you off your bike?' threatened Bridget as they rode away. It was no good, however. John Joe was laughing so hard that he almost fell off his bicycle by himself.

'Sorry,' he gulped, in the end. 'It was just funny. I was thinking of your face made out of bread-mix and currants, with a whole lot of carrots sticking out of it.'

Bridget rode dangerously near him, and he put on speed and went ahead of her up the hill. By the time she caught up with him, he had stopped laughing.

'Where is your da, then?' he asked. 'If he wasn't on the lorry and he isn't lying wounded, where is he?'

'I don't know,' said Bridget miserably.

'Maybe he'll be at home when you get there,' said John Joe consolingly.

Bridget shook her head. 'He won't be. I'm sure of that. He would never leave his men.'

Chapter Six

When Bridget and her mother walked down the avenue together to mass, they were hardly speaking to each other. It seemed to Bridget that her mother was worrying more about the inconvenience of milking the cows than about her husband's life; and Maggie despaired of making her daughter realise what she considered to be Mike's selfishness in risking his own life, and his family's safety, for the sake of an unrealistic dream. Each of them had given up trying to make the other understand, so there was a silence — a cold silence — between them.

At the church door they separated. Instead of joining her mother at the top of the church, Bridget slipped into a pew beside one of John Joe's aunts, the wife of one of the men who had been arrested by the Black and Tans. Mary O'Callaghan's face was white under her black shawl, and her eyes were red-rimmed. Bridget reached out and gave her hand a sympathetic squeeze. Mary returned the pressure gratefully, but said nothing.

The priest entered the church, and, under cover of the noise made by everyone standing up, Bridget whispered to Mary, 'Where have they taken him?'

'To Ennistymon. I'm going to see him this afternoon. He's being taken to Ennis Jail on Monday.'

Everyone knelt down and the church was quiet, except for the murmur of the priest's voice saying the prayers. Bridget hardly listened. The Latin words passed by her like the murmur of the river. She was in a fever of anxiety.

She waited until the rustle of people sitting down for the sermon could hide her voice. Then she whispered, 'Mary, do you know where my da is?'

Mary O'Callaghan looked at her in surprise. 'He must be with the rest of the men, in Ennistymon. Sure, isn't he the leader of them all?'

Bridget shook her head. 'I was there when they were caught, and my father wasn't with them.'

Right through the sermon, Mary was obviously thinking about the situation. When everyone stood up for the creed, she murmured in Bridget's ear, 'Come with me this afternoon. I'll take you and John Joe and pretend you're my children. We'll find out what happened to your da.'

The minute that mass was over, Bridget slipped out and went around the side of the church to wait for John Joe, who was one of the altar boys. As soon as he came out, she said quickly, 'Ask my mother if I can come with you and your Aunt Mary to Ennistymon this afternoon.'

I must find out what happened to Da, she thought, as she watched John Joe approach her mother. She moved up behind him. He had his best smile on, and, with his black hair neatly combed for mass, he looked quite handsome. Bridget knew her mother had a soft spot for John Joe; she always gave him cake when he came to the house, and she enjoyed his jokes and his flattery.

'Can Bridget come with me and Aunty Mary to

Ennistymon this afternoon, Mrs McMahon? She'll be back in good time.'

Maggie's eyes hardened, but she shrugged her shoulders. 'Bridget does what she likes, John Joe. She hardly ever bothers to ask for permission. Her father is away, and I'm left with all the cows to milk and the poultry to see to.'

'I'll come and help with the milking,' said John Joe gallantly. 'You won't be too long on your own, Mrs McMahon, I promise you that.'

Bridget moved away through the crowd and found Mary O'Callaghan. 'What time will you be going?' she asked in a low voice.

'About two o'clock,' replied Mary. 'I'll pick you and John Joe up at the crossroads.'

Bridget made sure that she was waiting at the gate by the crossroads well before two o'clock. John Joe wasn't long after her. While they were waiting for Mary, they discussed what they should do.

'You'd better put Aunty Mary's shawl around your head when you go into the barracks,' warned John Joe. 'If there are any Black and Tans around, they'll recognise your hair. It would be impossible to forget hair like that.'

Bridget pushed him off the gate, but her heart wasn't in it. She was too worried about her father to quarrel with John Joe. He was right, anyway, she knew; she would have to cover her head when she went in. She should have thought of that herself.

However, Mary's shawl covered her well, and when they reached the barracks there were no Black and Tans to be seen — only one fat policeman. Mary curtseyed deeply to him. Bridget looked at her in astonishment. All the way into Ennistymon, Mary had never ceased to abuse the police and the Black and Tans and the soldiers. Grown-up people are very good at hiding their feelings, thought Bridget, pulling Mary's black shawl closer around her face so that not one piece of red hair could be seen, just in case there was a Black and Tan looking out of the window.

'Could we see my husband, Patrick O'Callaghan, sir — please — just myself and my two children?'

'All right,' said the policeman curtly. 'Just for ten minutes.'

He brought them into the front office of the barracks and came back with Patrick. To Bridget's dismay, the policeman stayed in the room and watched them closely.

'No talking Irish, now,' he said sternly.

Bridget's heart sank. How could she ever ask Patrick about her father? It would be worse than useless; it would be downright dangerous.

If Patrick was surprised to find that John Joe and Bridget were supposed to be his children, he showed no sign of it; he chatted happily to them all. He's in very good spirits, thought Bridget, admiring his bravery. She could see that he had had a bad time. His face was covered in bruises, and he walked with a slight limp.

From time to time, Patrick O'Callaghan looked at Bridget consideringly, and her heart gave a slight leap; she understood that he had some news for her and didn't know how to give her it. She didn't know how to help; she could only look at him, powerless.

The ten minutes came to an end all too quickly. Just as they were going out, however, Patrick found his opportunity. He ruffled John Joe's hair playfully and advised him to do some fishing the next day —

'And take Bridget with you,' he added.

John Joe looked startled, and Patrick winked at him.

'There's some good trout in the valley of the apples,' he said in Irish. The policeman looked at him suspiciously. 'That's the name of a great fishing spot nearby, Sergeant,' said Patrick politely. 'Do you ever get a chance to cast a line yourself?'

The policeman grunted, but said no more. Clearly he was no longer suspicious. But John Joe, Mary and Bridget were all deeply puzzled. It was obviously meant to be a message about Bridget's father, or why should he have included her name? But where on earth was the valley of the apples?

All the way home, Bridget said the words over and over to herself; but it was only when she translated them into English that she suddenly understood.

'Applevale!' she shouted.

'Of course!' John Joe said. 'Why didn't we think of Applevale before?'

Applevale House was a ruined building on the Wilbrook road, a couple of miles from the station. It must once have been a beautiful house — huge, with about ten bedrooms, and a whole line of stables beside it — but now it was just a roofless ruin. It had been the scene of a terrible murder about a hundred years before, and people said that it was haunted. No one would go near it at night, and even in daylight people kept well away from its gloomy, ivy-covered walls.

'The men must have been hiding out there, in Applevale House,' said John Joe, 'and for some reason your da didn't go on the job with them. He must have been hurt.'

Bridget said nothing, but her face was white and her eyes were full of horror. Perhaps the men had been on another engagement and her father had been shot ....

'I don't think it's anything too bad,' said John Joe, understandingly. 'Uncle Patrick looked too happy for that. I'm sure he's all right. Maybe he's twisted an ankle.'

'I must go there tonight,' said Bridget resolutely.

'Your mam probably won't let you,' said John Joe. It was well known that Maggie McMahon was dead against the Irish Republican Army and was furious with her husband for getting mixed up with it. Still, John Joe thought, maybe it would be different if she knew he was injured.

He was just thinking that he would ask his mother if he could go with Bridget, when they heard an engine in the distance — and then, to their horror, came the sound of shots.

A lorry, driving far too fast for the dangerously narrow road, came skidding around one of the frequent bends. The lorry was full of Black and Tans, and they were obviously all drunk. They were singing obscene songs at the tops of their voices and leaning out of the lorry to shoot wildly at everything they could see — crows, cows, ponies, anything.

Luckily, they were so drunk that they hit nothing; but Mary O'Callaghan's Connemara pony, usually so steady and trustworthy, reared up when a shot whistled over his head, and then bolted down the hill as fast as he could go.

'Hang on to the reins, Aunty Mary!' shouted John Joe, clambering into the front of the cart. 'Whatever you do, don't let go of them!' Quickly he put his own hands on the reins as well, and leaned back as far as he could.

Bridget clung tightly to the side of the cart. For a while it looked as if the combined strengths of John Joe and his aunt might be enough to slow the pony; but it was no use. The road was narrow and full of potholes, and they were going downhill much too fast.

They had just reached the bottom of the hill when the inevitable happened: the harness straps broke, releasing the pony from the shafts; the cart tipped over into the ditch, and one of its wheels broke off; and the pony bolted for home.

'I'll kill them,' said John Joe, as he picked himself out of the ditch.

'Better join the IRA, then, if that's what you want to do,' said Bridget smartly.

John Joe didn't answer. He was bending over his aunt. She lay very still, and her face was chalk-white.

John Joe looked up with his eyes full of horror. 'Oh, my God,' he gasped. 'Do you think her neck is broken?'

Bridget bent over the unconscious woman. 'I don't know,' she said, her voice trembling.

She looked at Mary more carefully. 'I don't know,' she said again, 'but I don't think so. I've seen a hare with its neck broken, and it looked different. I think she just cracked her head on that big stone there. She's got a bad cut and she's bleeding a lot. I'll tear a bit off my petticoat and bandage it up.'

'I'll see if I can get some water,' said John Joe. 'I think there's a well back there, along the Ballagh road. Where the blazes has that pony gone? I'll keep shouting for him while I'm getting the water.'

Bridget could hear his voice all the time she was waiting. She kept touching Mary, to reassure herself that she was still alive. Mary remained warm, but deeply unconscious.

After what seemed like an hour, but was probably only about five minutes, John Joe returned with the water. They tried to get Mary to drink some, but it just trickled out of the corner of her mouth. John Joe looked at Bridget in despair.

'Let's try dabbing it on her forehead,' said Bridget. 'Have you got a clean handkerchief?'

'No,' said John Joe.

Bridget looked at her own handkerchief, but it was pretty filthy.

'We'll just pour a little over her head,' she decided. 'That might work just as well.'

She tried a few drops of water, but it had no effect.

'You're not christening her,' said John Joe impatiently. 'Just slosh it on.'

Bridget poured the water a bit faster, and, to their great relief, Mary's eyelids fluttered a little and she groaned slightly.

'Great!' said John Joe enthusiastically. 'Give it to me. I can always get some more.'

He dashed the rest of the cold water over Mary's forehead. This time she definitely opened her eyes and tried to lift her head.

'Well, her neck isn't broken, anyway,' said Bridget, with great relief.

'I'll run and get some more water,' said John Joe, setting off with his can at a great pace.

By the time he was back — and this time it didn't seem to take him nearly as long — Mary had regained consciousness. John Joe held the can to her lips and she drank thirstily.

'Hold my arms, the two of you, and I'll see if I can

sit up,' she said weakly.

She sat up successfully, but when she tried to stand, she sank back with a cry of agony.

'I think my ankle's broken,' she said. 'Now, how in the world can I get home? You'll have to catch the pony.'

'I've been trying,' said John Joe. 'There's no sign of him. Do you think he's gone home to his own stable?'

'It could be,' said Mary, sinking back and closing her eyes. Her face was very white.

Bridget and John Joe exchanged alarmed glances.

'I'd better go back to Ballinacarra,' said John Joe in a low tone. 'I'll see if the pony's there; if he's not, I'll just have to go to my cousin's place at Knockroe.'

'Better see if the cart is all right, first,' said Bridget. 'There's no point in bringing the pony if the cart's broken. Let's see if we can get it out of the ditch.'

Probably the cart would have been too heavy for Bridget and John Joe; but, in any case, one glance showed them that it would be useless even to try.

'One wheel is off, and the back axle's broken,' said John Joe, looking at it gloomily.

'Well, never mind,' said Bridget. 'We mightn't have been able to get her into it, anyway. You'd better go to your cousin in Knockroe and try to bring back someone to help us. I'll stay with Mary and look after her.'

'What about your mam?'

Bridget shrugged. 'What about yours?' she countered. 'I suppose everyone will be having a fit, but it's not our fault. They can blame the Black and Tans.'

Chapter Seven

It was after midnight by the time Bridget ran up the avenue to Drumshee. It had taken John Joe a long time to find his cousin, who had been out visiting neighbours. She was bruised all over, and she felt exhausted.

Maggie was almost hysterical; she had been convinced that her daughter, as well as her husband, had vanished for ever. It took Bridget a long time to calm her down enough to listen to the story.

'So you see, Mam,' she said finally, 'he must be injured. Patrick O'Callaghan was definitely giving me a message when he mentioned Applevale House, and he was hiding it from the policeman — he said it in Irish, although we always call it "Applevale House" even when we're speaking Irish. I think what must have happened is that Da was injured in some way and the men left him behind; they meant to pick him up when they'd finished the job on the railway line, but of course they couldn't, because the Black and Tans arrested them. It's too late to go and look for him now, so I'm going to get some sleep, and then I'll go up there on my bicycle in the morning.'

'You can't do that,' said Maggie, alarmed. 'The Black and Tans might catch you too!'

They already have, thought Bridget; but she decided

to keep that part of the story to herself. Her mother would never allow her out by herself again if she knew that Bridget had been left tied up and gagged under the trees at Wilbrook.

'I've asked John Joe to come with me,' she said. 'We'll be all right together. No one will question a pair of children. We'll take fishing-rods and a picnic basket with us. Da will need some food, anyway; he'll have been there by himself for two days.'

'Perhaps I should go too,' said Maggie reluctantly, a guilty look coming over her face.

'Well, you certainly can't ride a bicycle,' said Bridget cheerfully, 'and I don't think you could manage the pony either. John Joe and I will find Da, and he'll know the best thing to do next.'

Maggie sighed, and Bridget felt a pang of pity for her. I suppose it's not much fun being pregnant, she thought. Maybe Da should have put off the job at Wilbrook until she'd had the baby. Still, a patriot has to think of his country first of all. It's a good job Michael Collins isn't married, she thought sleepily.

She yawned widely and climbed up the ladder to her bedroom. Before she could think any more about her worries, she was asleep.

It seemed to Bridget that it was only a few minutes before her mother was shaking her awake. 'Bridget,' she was saying. 'Bridget, John Joe is here already. He's got his fishing-rod with him.'

Bridget sat up in a hurry. For a moment, she had an excited feeling; but then she remembered that this was a real adventure, not just playing about. At the thought of the rope which the Black and Tans had tied around her wrists and ankles, she gave a shiver.

However, this time she would have John Joe with

her. She threw back the bedclothes and began to dress as fast as she could.

'No rush,' said Maggie, turning with a weary sigh to climb back down the steep ladder. 'John Joe's gone to let out the poultry and milk the cows. What a nice boy he is — always so helpful and kind.'

Bridget smiled to herself as her mother went out. Whenever she went to the Arkinses' house, Mrs Arkins was always telling John Joe how helpful Bridget was and asking him why he couldn't be like that. Maybe we should swap families, she thought with a grin.

She had time to eat a quick breakfast before John Joe was back with the milk. Maggie had packed a picnic, with plenty of food for three people; and, without being asked, she had put in one of her herbal drinks for reducing fever and helping pain. She was in quite a good mood that morning — almost as if she were ashamed of all her complaints of the last few days.

Bridget, looking at the black shadows under the beautiful eyes, the weary, bent shoulders and the swollen ankles, also felt rather ashamed of her impatience. With a sudden surge of love, she kissed her mother.

'Don't worry, now,' she said affectionately. 'John Joe and I will be fine. We'll be back in a few hours.'

'Better not say that,' said Maggie, with a gallant effort at a smile. 'The last time you said that, it was dark before you arrived home. I'll expect you when I see you. John Joe says his brother is coming up to do the cows this evening, and I can do the poultry myself. It will help me to keep my mind off things.'

It had begun to rain slightly by the time Bridget

and John Joe were halfway up the road to Wilbrook; but, like most people in the west of Ireland, they took very little notice of rain. It was a warm day, and the rain felt pleasant on their hot cheeks as they cycled up the steep hills.

'You're getting really good at riding, Bridget,' said John Joe admiringly. 'You'll soon be as fast as me.'

'Oh, really?' said Bridget scathingly. 'How wonderful! Imagine being as fast as the marvellous John Joe Arkins! I could never hope to be as good as that.'

John Joe chuckled, grabbed a handful of sticky goosegrass from the hedge and stuffed it down the back of her dress. Bridget rode a little faster, right into the middle of a puddle, and had the satisfaction of splashing his trousers with wet mud. Her new bicycle had a mudguard on it, so she stayed dry.

She felt very cheerful. She was sure that this day was going to work out well. She had learned her lesson: she was going to imagine that there were Black and Tans behind every bush, and she was going to make sure that all they saw was two children going fishing for the day.

And so, when they got off their bicycles to walk up an especially steep hill, Bridget looked around carefully before saying anything. It was almost mountainous here, and the land on either side of the road was bare and rocky. There were no hedges that anyone could be hiding behind; there was no possibility that anyone could overhear them.

'What's the plan, then?' asked John Joe in a low voice.

'Well,' said Bridget, 'I think we should leave our bicycles a good way away from Applevale House and cross the fields to the river. We'll sit down and do some fishing for about half an hour. Then we'll talk very loudly about there being no fish there, and we'll move further along until we're nearly opposite Applevale House and do some more fishing. Then I'll go off into the bushes and sneak around the back, into the house. You stay there, fishing.'

'No, I won't,' said John Joe decisively. 'I told your mother I'd look after you, and I'm coming with you. Goodness knows what might be at Applevale House.'

'I'm not afraid of ghosts, if that's what you're thinking,' said Bridget angrily. Then she gave in. 'Oh, all right, then,' she said. 'I suppose by then we'll be sure that no one's watching. I know now how the Black and Tans disguise themselves: they put branches on their hats and tie them over their uniforms.'

'Right,' said John Joe. 'As soon as I see a branch moving across the field, I'll cast the fishing-line at it and catch myself a Black and Tan.'

'Better not,' said Bridget, with a giggle. 'They'd probably do worse to you than just tie you up. Anyway, let's not talk about it any more. You can bore me by telling me all about the best way of fishing, and I'll just go on planning in my mind.'

~

It's agony to be just sitting here, fishing, thought Bridget half an hour later, as they sat beside the little river. It's a good job John Joe's with me; otherwise I'd probably have abandoned my plan and gone straight to Applevale House.

Pretending she was keeping an eye on the float, she cautiously half-turned and looked at the huge building, black against the skyline. No wonder people said it was haunted. Its walls towered at least forty feet high, and every inch of wall was smothered in thick, dark-green ivy.

With difficulty, Bridget turned her glance away. Foot by foot, she was checking all the nearby ground. All around them were green fields, gently sloping towards the river, with no trace of cover in any of them. The cattle were all grazing peacefully; it was unlikely they would be so calm if anyone strange was near them. The only place Bridget wasn't sure about was a disused quarry between the river and Applevale House. It was so overgrown with brambles and other plants that it was hard to be sure whether it was empty or not.

Bridget put down her fishing-rod.

'Did you see that butterfly, John Joe?' she asked, in a high, excited voice. 'I've never seen a butterfly like that before! It went into the quarry up there. I'm just going to have a look. I might be able to catch it for my collection.'

Praying that John Joe wouldn't say, 'But you don't collect butterflies, you told me it was cruel,' Bridget moved quickly across the grass into the quarry. It wasn't as overgrown as she had feared, and she found that she could easily move around it. There were lots of butterflies there, funnily enough, but there were certainly no Black and Tans or soldiers.

'I'm getting bored with this place,' she complained loudly, when she returned to John Joe. 'Let's go further along and see if we can catch any fish there.'

'All right,' said John Joe, entering into the spirit of things. 'But it's no wonder I can't catch any fish. You keep fidgeting and talking; you're scaring the fish away. Why don't you go off for a walk? But make sure you come back in ten minutes. If you don't, I'll have to come after you. I promised your mother I'd look after you.'

Bridget suppressed a quick smile. This was perfect. She really didn't want to waste any more time sitting by that river. She was pretty convinced that there were no Black and Tans around, anyway. She dumped her rod on the ground next to John Joe and set off up the steep hill, keeping well inside the shelter of the blackthorn bushes and going in the opposite direction to Applevale House.

Only when Bridget was high on the hill above Applevale House did she dare to turn towards the west again and make her way carefully down towards the ruin. No one would be able to see her from the road, and by now she was sure that no one was hiding nearby. After all, why would the Black and Tans be hiding out on the hillside in the rain? It wasn't like that time when they'd been waiting for the ambush of the train. No, Bridget was pretty sure that she and John Joe were the only people around — so it came as even more of a shock when suddenly a hand was clapped over her mouth.

For a moment, her heart seemed to stop; but then she realised that the hand wasn't much bigger than her own. Furious with herself as well as with John Joe, Bridget twisted around and met the brown eyes — not laughing now, but deadly serious.

With his finger on his lips, John Joe took his hand off her mouth and, beckoning with his head, moved cautiously towards the edge of a little wood. Bridget followed, moving as carefully as he did, and peered through the tangled hazel branches.

Then she saw why John Joe was being so careful.

Out in the fields was a farmer inspecting his cattle; and, even worse, he had a dog with him.

The dog could obviously smell the children's presence in the air. Every few minutes he got to his feet and started to go up the hill towards them, and every few minutes he was roared at ferociously by his master.

'Sit down!' the farmer yelled angrily, again and again. And again and again, to Bridget's and John Joe's relief, the dog reluctantly sat down. Neither of them dared to move. The dog was obviously not very well trained, and any movement would undoubtedly have sent him flying at them.

Bridget felt wild with impatience. They had wasted the whole morning pretending to fish, and now there was this new delay. Perhaps her father had nothing to eat with him — or, worse still, nothing to drink. Perhaps he was badly hurt, losing blood ....

She almost felt like taking a chance — but she restrained herself, remembering what had happened to Patrick O'Callaghan. The last thing she wanted to do was to lead anyone, anyone at all, to her father's hiding-place. Not everyone sympathised with the aims of the IRA, her father had told her. 'They want Ireland to be free,' he had said bitterly, 'but they don't want to take any trouble over it. They want to lead their lives peacefully and let the politicians get on with talks over in London. They don't realise that no one would be bothered talking if there wasn't a threat behind the talks.' Bridget could almost hear his voice in her ears, saying, 'We have to expect every man's hand to be against us.' She looked at the farmer and his eager dog and decided that patience was the only answer.

Chapter Seven

It took the farmer half an hour to check his cattle; but to Bridget and John Joe it seemed like hours. When he finally left, dragging his dog with him, they moved with more caution than ever, stopping every few minutes to look and listen.

Seen from close by, Applevale House was even bigger than it had seemed from a distance. Somehow they hadn't expected it to be so huge. There was a door at the back, but the lock seemed to be rusted into the timber; they decided against trying to force it and went timidly around to the front, keeping close to the ivy-covered walls. The front door was also closed, but the front windows were long gone.

'Look,' said John Joe, in a whisper. 'It looks as if someone climbed in this window, not long ago. See the bits of ivy torn away? And there are footprints in the dust inside.'

'You're right,' said Bridget. 'I was thinking they'd have gone in at the back, but of course they went in there in the middle of the night, so they wouldn't have worried about anyone seeing them. You keep watch while I climb in, and then wait a moment until I give you the word.'

Feeling hopeful again, Bridget climbed over the low windowsill and into a huge room, open to the sky. Carefully she looked out of the window, down the hill towards the West Clare Railway line. She could see no one, so she whispered, 'Come on,' and John Joe followed her in.

'Let's follow the footprints,' he said. 'You can see them quite clearly.'

Once they reached the centre of the house, however, the light was too poor to see anything much. They wandered here and there for ages, until something

made Bridget try a half-rotten old door, set in a wall
and almost invisible — it, too, was covered with ivy.
In fact, what caught her eye was some newly broken-
off pieces of ivy lying at its foot.

She pushed the door gently, and it opened. Behind
it was a flight of steps.

'We should have brought a candle,' whispered
John Joe. 'Take care, the stairs are probably rotten.'

As they crept down the stairs, Bridget thought she
heard a sound — a sound like someone drawing in a
breath — but she said nothing. It was only when she
reached the bottom, and a shaft of sunlight suddenly
shone down the stairway and lit up her hair, that her
father spoke.

'How in the name of God did you two find me?'

Mike McMahon was not starving, as Bridget had
feared he would be. Nevertheless, after lasting for
two days on some stale bread, he was delighted to
see a hearty meal.

'How's your mam?' was his first question, after they
had told him all about what they had overheard at
Ennistymon barracks, about the men being captured
by the Black and Tans and about Patrick O'Callaghan's
message.

'Oh, she's all right,' said Bridget impatiently. 'But
she's not too pleased,' she added with a giggle.

Mike sighed and stirred restlessly. 'I'm not sure I
blame her,' he said, trying to suppress a groan of pain.

Immediately Bridget forgot all about her mother.
'Oh, Da, are you hurt?' she cried. 'What happened
to you?'

'I'm all right,' Mike said. 'I just hurt my leg when
we were trying to roll a stone down next to the line.
Look, there's a candle and some matches there in the

box next to me. Light it and you'll see.'

With trembling hands, Bridget tried to strike a match. After the third one had gone out, John Joe silently took the box from her and lit the candle.

Mike didn't look well. He had black shadows under his eyes, and his unshaven face was drawn with pain. A piece of wood — it looked like a stake from someone's fence — was tied tightly to his leg, which was stretched out awkwardly in front of him.

'Is it broken?' asked John Joe quietly.

Mike shrugged his shoulders. 'Probably,' he said. 'Don't worry, Bridget, it'll soon mend. I've had many a broken bone in my life. The only thing I can do now, I think, is to lie up here for a few days. What did that fellow at the barracks look like, Bridget?'

'He had black hair, sort of sticking up from his head, and ears the shape of jug-handles,' said Bridget. 'I think he was quite small, too.'

'Sounds like Curtin,' said her father grimly. 'Michael Collins warned me about him. Well, if that little rat has told the Black and Tans that there were ten men, they'll be looking for me. I don't think he knows my name, though — I hope not, anyway. I think you two had better go now. Take care of your mother, Bridget; she's not up to doing much work now, with the baby due so soon. Tell her I'm sorry about this — but, who knows, peace might come one day .... Bring me some food tomorrow, and a book, if you can. Do the same as you did today: spend most of the morning fishing. Be very careful not to lead them to me. They have spies everywhere. And I don't want them taking me here, like a rat in a trap.'

Chapter Eight

Tuesday 5 July 1921

I'll never be able to fish again in my life, thought Bridget, as she sat beside the stream and watched John Joe lift his rod and snake the line out into the middle of the water. She was tired of doing that herself. She was too worried to concentrate, and time after time her line had snagged in the long grasses and reeds or in the overhanging branches. She sat lethargically, watching the sun move high in the summer sky.

'You'd better look as if you're enjoying yourself,' said John Joe in a low voice. 'After all, nobody's going to believe that you'd cycle all the way up to Wilbrook just for the pleasure of scrambling around the hillside, so if anyone's keeping a lookout, we have to look like mad keen fishermen.'

Bridget sighed and impatiently reeled in her line. Nothing on it, as she had guessed. Still, she supposed, it was easier to keep reeling it in and trying to throw it out again than to think about her father. She even managed to put on an air of enthusiasm when John Joe caught his sixth fish of the morning. But she was glad when the sun reached its height and John Joe decided it was safe to leave the fishing for a while and bring the food to Mike.

They had brought candles and matches, so John

Joe lit a candle before they went down the stairs of Applevale House. As they opened the door to the stairway, they were taken aback to hear Mike's voice. He didn't sound as if he was talking to someone — more as if he was muttering to himself. John Joe looked at Bridget in surprise.

'Maybe he's saying poetry to himself, to pass the time,' said Bridget. 'He loves poetry.'

It wasn't poetry that Mike was saying, however; it was a string of meaningless, unintelligible phrases. Bridget looked at him in alarm. He was lying on his back, his face very flushed and his lips dry and cracked. She put her hand on his forehead; it was boiling hot.

'Oh, John Joe,' she said in alarm, 'he's got a fever. He's very sick. What will we do?'

'Did he take any of the fever medicine that your mother gave you for him?' asked John Joe.

Bridget shone the candle into the tin box beside her father. 'I don't think so,' she said. 'There's none gone that I can see.'

'Well, try giving him some now,' advised John Joe.

Bridget sat down on the cold, damp stone floor and took her father's head on her lap. He was lying on a sort of bed of grass and heather and bracken, but even so, he must have been desperately chilled during the last few days. She hoped fervently that he was suffering from a cold or from influenza — that the fever wasn't the result of something seriously wrong with his leg.

He was tossing his head from side to side, making it very difficult for her to get the liquid into his mouth, but eventually she managed it.

'I wish we had a clock,' she said aloud. 'I think

70

this stuff should work in about an hour.'

'I'll make you a clock,' said John Joe, glad of the opportunity to do something rather than standing around feeling helpless. 'Just wait a minute. I won't be long.'

After about five minutes, John Joe was back with a few long rushes and a blackthorn twig with several long thorns on it.

'Look,' he said. 'This is a four-hour candle, right?'

'Right,' said Bridget, wondering what was coming next.

'Well, I'm going to measure it with this piece of rush, and then fold the rush into four and use it to mark the candle with my knife; each quarter should last an hour. Now I'll stick a thorn into each of the three lines. After an hour, one thorn will fall out, and so on. After four hours, the whole candle will have burned out. I'll put it in the tin, so it's not in a draught.'

'That's very clever,' said Bridget admiringly.

Watching the candle helped to pass the time a bit, but still, it was a long hour before the first thorn fell out. John Joe fetched some water from the stream so that Bridget could bathe her father's burning face and neck, but by the end of the hour, he was no better. Carefully, Bridget managed to spoon another dose of her mother's medicine into him.

Then she stood up, with an air of determination.

'He needs a doctor,' she said. 'I'm going to Corofin to get one for him.'

John Joe gasped. 'How can you get a doctor?' he said. 'A doctor would never come here. And how could you pay him if he did?'

'We'll offer him your fish,' said Bridget confidently.

'After all, there are six trout in your basket down in the river. That should make a nice dinner for him.'

'And what happens if he tells the Black and Tans where your father is?'

'Oh, I'll swear him to secrecy before I tell him anything. Let's go. I'll leave the candle burning, so we'll know how long we've been away.'

John Joe looked doubtful, but he said nothing. He had never heard of anyone paying a doctor with half a dozen trout. However, he was used to doing what Bridget told him, so he didn't argue; he just followed her back up the stairs and out into the sunlight. They went back to the river and collected the trout, then took their bicycles from under the hedge.

Corofin was only a few miles away, and it was downhill a lot of the way. It was two o'clock by the church clock when they reached the main street. The doctor was obviously just finishing his midday meal when they arrived; he came to the door wiping his mouth on a linen napkin.

'What do you want?' he asked abruptly, waving aside the trim maid in her white cap and black dress.

'My father is very sick,' said Bridget. 'He's broken his leg and he has a bad fever.'

The doctor sighed. 'Well, I'd better come and see him,' he said. 'Where does he live?'

Bridget hesitated. Better get the easy bit over first, she thought.

'We don't have any money to pay you, sir,' she said. 'Would you come if we gave you these trout?'

The doctor's eyebrows shot up, and the maid gave a stifled giggle. Bridget shot her a venomous glance. Anyone who wears a silly cap like that, she said silently to the maid, has no right to laugh at anyone else. However, she said nothing. John Joe silently held out the basket of trout so that the doctor could inspect them.

'When did you catch them?'

'They were all caught this morning, sir, and I've been keeping them cool in the river. They're as fresh as can be.'

The doctor looked carefully at the shining fish and then nodded his head, a smile on his face. 'Very well, then,' he said crisply. 'Now tell me where you live.'

Bridget took a deep breath and clasped her hands together nervously. 'Before I tell you,' she said, 'will you swear not to tell anyone about my father — where he is, or how he got hurt?'

The doctor looked puzzled. Then his face darkened.

'Ah, so he's one of those ruffians who were trying to derail the train,' he said. 'I'm sorry, young lady, but I'll have nothing to do with a man like that. The RIC are out looking for him, you know. They were asking around the houses in Corofin yesterday.'

Bridget's face went as white as chalk. Without a word, she stepped back and slammed the front door in the doctor's astonished face. Then she grabbed John Joe by the hand and set off running down the path. They both jumped on their bicycles and ped-alled, as fast as they could, down a side road. In the distance they heard the maid shouting, 'Come back,' and then the doctor's voice saying impatiently, 'Oh, never mind them. I'm going back to my dinner.'

All the same, neither Bridget nor John Joe stopped to draw breath until they were halfway back to Wilbrook. Then they had to get off their bicycles, to walk up a steep hill; but there was no sign of any pursuit, so they began to feel reasonably safe.

'Well, that's that, then,' said Bridget. 'I was stupid even to think of it.'

'What are you going to do now?' asked John Joe curiously.

'I don't know,' said Bridget.

Her face was wet with tears, so John Joe didn't say any more.

They reached the wall near the river. After hiding their bicycles behind a thick hazel bush and replacing the fish in the fast-flowing water, they cautiously made their way back to Applevale House.

As they came to the door at the top of the stairs, they could see the light from the candle, but there was no sound from Mike.

John Joe looked at the candle. 'We've been gone about an hour and a half,' he said.

But Bridget wasn't listening. She was looking at her father. He was lying very still, and there was no longer a flush on his face. He looked like a piece of marble.

Bridget touched him. He was definitely cooler, and when she looked at him closely, she saw that he was sleeping peacefully. A great feeling of relief came over her.

'I'm going to stay here with him tonight, John Joe,' she said. 'The medicine is doing him good, but he's too sick to remember to take it himself. If you mark out some more candles for me, then I can give it to him every two hours, right through the night, and he might be a lot better by the morning.'

'Do you want me to stay with you?' asked John Joe.

'No, you must go back and tell Mam where I am, or she'll have a fit. Anyway, we'll have to get him home tomorrow. He can't stay here any longer or he might get even sicker, and it's too dangerous anyway. You heard what that foul doctor said: "The RIC are looking for him."'

John Joe chuckled — Bridget had said the last sentence in the precise Anglo-Irish tones of the doctor — but then he grew serious again.

'How on earth can we get him back home? He has a broken leg.'

'Well, that's where you come in. I want you to bring our cart — the pony's very quiet and easy to manage, and if you fill the cart with hay, we'll be able to hide my father under the hay and get him home without anyone being any the wiser. If you get stopped on the way here, you can just say you're bringing some hay to bed down a newborn calf.'

'And if we get stopped on the way back?'

Bridget shrugged. 'We won't. Anyway, I have to take the chance. They know there was another man, and he could easily be found here, once they really begin to search. You don't need to come back with us. You can bring your bicycle on the cart, and stay here and do some more fishing until we're well out of the way.'

'Don't be stupid,' said John Joe roughly. 'I'm not scared. I'm just trying to think about things, instead of just rushing ahead and doing them, like you.'

Bridget felt herself flare up with anger, but she suppressed it. John Joe was right. That visit to the doctor had been really stupid, and they had been lucky to get out of it so easily.

After a moment, she said meekly, 'Well, all right, what would you do?'

John Joe shrugged his shoulders. 'Actually, I think it's quite a good plan. I'll try and make some sort of

frame tonight, so we can heap the hay over your
da without smothering him. Well, see you in the
morning, Carrots. Have a good night. Watch out for
the ghosts.'

Bridget grinned to herself as John Joe went out.
He was infuriating, but he was always good fun. She
was glad he was going to make the journey with her
the next day.

She turned her attention to her father. She thought
he was even cooler now than he had been when they
came back. Soon it would be time for another dose of
the medicine, and then she might be able to get him
to eat and drink something. All the neighbours
thought very highly of Maggie's medicines. Probably
they would do Mike just as much good as a doctor
would have.

Chapter Nine

Bridget slept very little that night, and never once neglected to give her father his medicine every two hours. He slept most of the night, but at about five in the morning he woke up and, to Bridget's great joy, took some milk and some bread and honey. They sat there, talking companionably, while the ray of sunshine coming in through the high window grew brighter.

'You see, Bridget,' said Mike, 'your mother can't understand why I'm still doing this, now that I have a family to take care of. There are times when I don't understand myself. I wish I hadn't gone for this job; but a big consignment of arms and ammunition was being transported by the West Clare Railway line, and the people of Ennistymon and Miltown Malbay have suffered enough with the Black and Tans driving around and letting off their guns for no reason.'

'I understand,' said Bridget, and she told him about the Black and Tans' lorry driving Mary O'Callaghan's cart off the road. 'I think that changed John Joe's ideas,' she added. 'Before that, he was very against the IRA — or at least his mother was.'

'He's a nice lad, John Joe. They're a nice family altogether — good neighbours. What time are you expecting him?'

'He said he'd come as early as possible, so no one

77

would see him. It should be any time now, I think. I'll go out and have a look.'

Bridget went outside, looking carefully through the window before climbing out. The air was cool, but she could see that it was going to be a nice day. Everything was very quiet, so when the cart came rumbling up the hill towards Wilbrook it sounded very loud to her anxiously listening ears. With another quick look around, she slipped across the field, keeping close to the shady side of the hedge, and was waiting when John Joe pulled the pony to a halt.

He had filled the cart with loose hay, and he proudly showed her the results of his work the night before. He had bored holes in two long, narrow pieces of wood, then bent small, flexible branches of willow into the holes; the result was rather like a man-sized, bottom-less lobster-pot. He had brought a tarpaulin to cover it; the hay could then be stacked on top of the tarpaulin.

'We'll leave it open near his head, so he can breathe properly, and if we meet anyone you can just pull it into place,' said John Joe, clearly pleased at Bridget's approval. 'Look what else I made last night.' From under the hay he took another piece of wood, narrow at one end and with a triangular piece, well padded with old rags, at the other end.

'What's that for?' asked Bridget, puzzled.

'That's a crutch, to help him walk. It's like the one that the old fellow in Ennistymon has, the one who fought in the Great War. Do you remember seeing him? He gets around very fast with it. Remember the day we saw him chase after those children who were laughing at him? He could run nearly as fast as they could.'

'I think that's great,' said Bridget. 'You're good at making things, John Joe. Do you want to be a carpenter when you grow up?'

'I might,' said John Joe carelessly. 'Anyway, let's get your da out of that cellar before anyone comes.'

Mike was delighted with the crutch. He found that, once he was outside the house, he could manage without help. John Joe kept a hand on his other arm, just in case, and Bridget carried the tin with the candles and everything else in it. She had made absolutely sure that there was no sign left that someone had stayed in the cellar for a few days. She had carried out the bedding and spread it under the hedge, where the cows usually gathered when the sun reached its height. They would trample it into the mud, and after a day there would be no sign of it.

When they reached the cart, they had a terrible job getting Mike into it. He was a big, heavy man, so there was no possibility of Bridget and John Joe being able to hoist him up into it. In the end, John Joe removed the tailboard and Mike lay on the edge of the cart; then Bridget lifted his legs up and John Joe tugged his arms to help him drag himself into the cart. By the time he was in, Mike was groaning and sweating with agony, and Bridget looked almost as pale as her father.

Still, he was in. They put John Joe's wooden frame and the tarpaulin over him, and heaped hay over the top. Bridget sat beside her father, and John Joe climbed into the driver's seat and clicked his tongue at the pony.

John Joe drove the pony slowly along the Wilbrook road. Bridget knew that he was trying to save her father from too much jolting, but her nerves were so on edge that she wanted to scream at him to hurry up.

At the crossroads, both she and John Joe had to get out; the hill was too steep for the pony to climb pulling their extra weight. John Joe held the reins and led the pony along, coaxing it all the way. Bridget walked beside the cart, keeping an eye on her father, ready to draw the tarpaulin over his head if anyone appeared.

The hill seemed endless. The pony was getting old, and the combined weight of the cart, the hay and the man seemed too much for him. John Joe had to stop every few yards to give the pony time to breathe.

'Don't rush him,' came Mike's voice, slightly muffled by the hay. 'That pony is older than the two of you put together. I don't want him dropping down with a heart attack.'

A new worry began in Bridget's mind. She didn't know what they would do if anything did happen to the pony and they were stranded on the mountainy road. She stopped trying to urge John Joe to go faster and plodded patiently beside the cart until they reached the top of the hill. From there they could see for miles around. The whole landscape looked empty. Of course, it was probably only about half past six in the morning, and not many people would be up at that time.

When they started to go downhill, Bridget and John Joe got back into the cart, and the pony trotted along happily. Still, Bridget was the one who suggested that they should both get out again at the next hill. It wasn't much of a hill, but she was determined to spare the pony as much as possible.

They were about halfway up that hill when they heard the sound of a lorry revving as it climbed the steep hill behind them. Bridget looked at John Joe in alarm. There weren't many lorries in this quiet district, and certainly half past six in the morning wasn't the usual time to meet one.

'Quick,' said John Joe, in a low voice. 'Go through

the ditch. Hide behind that hedge. If they see you, they'll remember your hair.'

Faster than any fox, Bridget crossed the ditch and slipped behind the hedge. As she did so, she suddenly remembered that her father's face had been left almost uncovered. She peered through the hedge, in an agony.

'John Joe,' she whispered.

There was no answer. The wind was blowing her words back to her, and the grinding of gears from the lorry was so loud that, even if she had shouted, John Joe might not have heard her. She didn't dare shout, however. A shout might catch the attention of the Black and Tans. With all her strength, she willed John Joe to think of it; and, almost immediately, she saw him lean over casually and pull at the hay. Mike was completely covered.

'Keep down,' John Joe said in a low voice, the wind blowing the sound towards Bridget. 'I can see your hair through the hedge.'

This hair! thought Bridget. It's been the curse of my life since I was born. She crouched down. Then she had an idea. The ditch below her was full of wet mud. She plunged her hands into it and plastered the thick mud all over her head, rubbing it into her hair as if she were shampooing it. For good measure, she also rubbed some mud over her face, so that its whiteness wouldn't show up.

The lorry was coming down the first hill. Soon it would catch up with John Joe, still plodding slowly up the second hill. It drew level with Bridget. She held her breath.

The next moment she gasped in horror. A shot had whistled over her head. They must have seen her!

Bridget crouched as low as she could, hiding her head in her hands and waiting for shouts and more shots. The lorry was stopping; she could hear the wheels grinding to a halt. She turned her face away from the road, still desperately hoping that she might not be seen.

She looked across the field and felt a sudden spark of hope. Lying dead, not a hundred yards from her, was a crow. Perhaps the Black and Tans hadn't seen her after all. They were always firing at something. A crow would do if there was nothing better.

The lorry, however, had definitely stopped. Bridget could hear a harsh voice shouting at John Joe, 'Here, you! Do you live around here?'

'Yes,' said John Joe. His voice sounded quite steady. Bridget felt proud of him. He's a great friend, she thought. I'll never fight with him again.

'Have you seen a man around here anywhere, hiding in an old shed or anything?'

John Joe said nothing. Go on, answer, screamed Bridget in her mind. Why is he always so slow?

'No,' said John Joe eventually. He managed to sound quite bewildered.

'Oh, come on,' said one of the men. 'They're all halfwits around here. Let's get back to Ennistymon. We're off duty in an hour, and then it's breakfast and bed for us all. I hate these night patrols. I always think there are IRA men behind every haystack.'

The lorry started up again, and the stink of exhaust fumes filled Bridget's nostrils, overwhelming the smell of mud and stagnant ditch-water. The lorry continued up to the top of the hill and changed gear for the descent. Bridget didn't dare to come out yet, but she began to walk up the field, keeping close to the hedge. John Joe was still leading the pony up the hill. He reached the top and stood there, waiting for Bridget. She quickened her pace and finally came out of the hedge, peering anxiously ahead to make sure that there was no sign of the lorry.

'Oh, my God!' sniggered John Joe, when he caught sight of her. 'It's a monster from the slimy depths! Help me, someone!'

'Oh, shut up,' snapped Bridget. 'You always think you're so clever and so funny. You're just a stupid little boy. Why didn't you answer that Black and Tan a bit more quickly? I thought you'd lost your tongue.'

'Now then, you two,' came Mike's muffled voice, from under the hay. 'How about trying to get me back to Drumshee, and saving the fight for later?'

'Oh, Da,' said Bridget, rushing around to free his mouth from the tarpaulin. 'Are you all right?'

Her father, however, began to chuckle when he saw her. 'I have to say, you do look a bit like a monster,' he said unfeelingly. 'There's a well a bit further along this road. You'd better stop and wash that stuff off. Your mother will have a fit if she sees you like that.'

So they stopped at the well, and John Joe scooped up a few pailfuls of water and Bridget rinsed her hair as well as she could.

'Does it look all right now?' she asked John Joe.

'Yes,' he said. 'It's red again. It suits you, red,' he added hastily, as he saw her colour begin to rise. 'I don't think I'd like black hair on you.'

'Thanks,' said Bridget awkwardly.

'Some people like red hair, you know. My cousin who came over from America last summer said that you had the most beautiful hair he'd ever seen,' John Joe went on.

'Really?'

'Yes, really. He said that out in America that sort of red is really fashionable.'

'You don't say!' said Bridget, her eyes glowing with excitement. 'I think I'll go out to America when I'm grown up. My cousin Kitty lives out there. She's married to a man from Corofin.'

'I might go, too,' said John Joe. 'My cousin has a building business out there. I could get trained as a carpenter. Anyway, you look fine now. Let's get your father back home.'

'Well, at least it's downhill all the way from here to Drumshee,' said Bridget thankfully.

They had only another mile to go, but Bridget was on edge all the way, watching and listening for any sign of the Black and Tans coming back. When they reached the gate to Drumshee, she leaned across to John Joe and said in a low voice, 'Just take the cart up the lane towards your own house and then wait for a minute. I'll run up the hill, across the Togher Field, and make sure there's no one around. I'm just worried that there might be some Black and Tans lying in wait for him, or something.'

'I don't think that's likely,' said John Joe reassuringly. 'If they'd known his name and where he lived, they'd have asked me about him, not just mentioned "a man".'

'Well, just in case,' said Bridget impatiently, climbing down from the cart. 'Anyway, I'll be able to wake Mam up and make sure everything's ready for him.'

Without arguing any more, John Joe did as he was told and drove the cart up the lane. Bridget ran through the gate and up the steep Togher Field as fast as she could. She passed the fort and thought briefly about the souterrain. Perhaps it would be safer to put her father there? But then she thought of what John Joe had said and decided that he was right. The Black and Tans just knew that one man was missing; they didn't know who it was. In any case, Mike needed a few days in a warm, dry, comfortable bed, with some good nursing.

When she reached the cottage, she was glad to see smoke coming from the chimney. Mam must be up, she thought. She opened the door, feeling a little apprehensive. What sort of mood would her mother be in? Would she blame Bridget for being out all night?

However, she needn't have worried; Maggie was only concerned about her husband.

'Oh, Bridget,' she said, as soon as Bridget appeared, 'where is he? Couldn't you bring him? John Joe said he'd be here by seven o'clock. Is he still feverish? John Joe said he was raving ....'

'He's all right,' said Bridget happily. 'He's much better. Your medicine worked really well. I was just checking that everything was all right before we brought him up the avenue.'

'You're a grand girl,' said Maggie, giving Bridget a kiss. 'Where would we be without you? Sure, you have more sense than either of us.'

Feeling blissfully happy, Bridget ran down the avenue and opened the gate. John Joe had seen her coming; he had turned the pony and was leading him back down the lane.

'Everything all right?' he asked.

'Everything's fine,' said Bridget. 'Let's get him into bed as fast as we can.'

Chapter Ten

Mike slept for most of Wednesday, and by Thursday morning he was looking much better. Maggie was in her element; she loved to nurse, and her herbal medicines were famous all over the neighbourhood. Usually Mike was too impatient to stay in bed when he was ill, but now he was so conscious of the dreadful anxiety he had inflicted on his wife that he lay there as patiently as he could, allowing himself to be cared for like a baby. Bridget, with John Joe and one of his brothers to help her, did all the outside work, and for once she enjoyed it.

'At least it's better than fishing,' she said. 'I don't ever want to go fishing again.'

'That reminds me,' said John Joe, as he carried a pail of milk into the house. 'I never went back to get those trout. They're still there in the river. I might as well have given them to that nice doctor after all.'

'Nice!' said Bridget, her face getting red with temper. Then she saw the grin on the corners of John Joe's mouth, so she contented herself with kicking him sharply in the ankle and making him spill some of the milk over his trousers.

'Oh, dear, John Joe, do be careful of the milk,' said Maggie, coming out of the bedroom.

Bridget grinned wickedly. She sometimes got a bit

sick of hearing what a marvel John Joe was.

'Bridget,' called Mike.

'Yes, Da?' said Bridget, going into the bedroom and noticing happily how much better he was looking.

'Bridget, I wondered if you and John Joe would like a day on the bog. That turf needs to be footed, or we'll have nothing to burn in the fire this winter. You could go on your bicycles and bring a picnic with you. It's lovely weather, just right for the bog, and your mother's just made a cake. You could take that with you.'

Bridget nodded. She wasn't mad about the bog, but at least it was in the opposite direction to Wilbrook. She felt as if she never wanted to see Wilbrook again.

To her surprise, John Joe was very enthusiastic when she asked him about going to the bog.

'I love the bog,' he said. 'And all of my family are going this afternoon, anyway. We'll have a great time. Let's go now. I'll borrow Da's bicycle again, and we might get a ride back in the evening.'

It didn't take them long to get ready. Bridget packed the picnic into her basket, while John Joe ran down the hill to his own house to tell his mother and to borrow the bicycle from his long-suffering father. The bog was on the far side of Kilfenora, so they had quite a long ride, but neither of them minded. It was lovely to cycle along without worrying about anything.

When they arrived at the bog, it was like a Fair Day; there were dozens of people there. A few were still footing their turf — picking up four damp sods at a time and leaning the narrow edges together so that the air could blow through and dry them. Most people, however, were already stacking the dry turf by the roadside, ready for collection by horses and carts, or else going over to their neighbours' plots and saying, 'God bless the work,' and laughing and singing songs.

The Arkins family arrived just after Bridget and John Joe had finished their picnic, and then it was even more fun. John Joe's family made a pet of him, since he was the youngest by seven years, and they were inclined to do the same to Bridget.

Mrs Arkins suspected that there was something wrong in the McMahon household, and she doubted John Joe's story about Mike being away helping his cousin in Galway. Whatever the problem was, however, she was sorry for the family, and she immediately sent over some of her big lads to help with the McMahons' turf. Bridget had already noticed that their plot had less work done on it than any of the others. Probably, when Mike had told Maggie he was footing the turf, he had actually been off on IRA business.

When the sun began to sink in the sky over the sea, Mrs Arkins stopped work, lit a little fire and put a kettle on to boil. When the tea was ready, she called them all over, and they sat on a bank of springy dry peat and wolfed down all the bread and scones and jam that they could fit in.

'I'm always starving at the bog,' said John Joe.

'It can't be the work,' said his eldest brother, David. 'I didn't see you do too much. You probably stacked about ten sods.'

'You don't know what you're talking about,' said John Joe, biting into his sixth scone. 'Bridget and I had a day's work done before you lot arrived.'

'This is the best day I've ever had at the bog,' said Bridget, looking longingly at the last scone on the cloth and wondering whether it would be bad manners to ask if anyone wanted it.

'Have another scone, pet,' said Mrs Arkins at that very moment. 'Sure, why wouldn't you enjoy yourself today, with all the other children? It's lonely work being an only child. Wait till your little brother or sister is here, and see what fun you'll have.'

Bridget said nothing, but a little warm feeling began to grow inside her. She hadn't really been looking forward to this baby, but Mrs Arkins was right: it was a bit lonely and serious being an only child. In two years' time her little brother or sister would be old enough to come to the bog.

The light was beginning to fade when everyone stopped work and packed the baskets and the kettle onto the cart. Bridget's and John Joe's bicycles were tied onto the back, and they climbed up and sat squashed in with all the rest of the Arkins family. All the way home, Bridget chatted happily with Mrs Arkins about the new baby. Suddenly she realised that she knew very little about babies, and she had a hundred questions. When would the baby start to walk, to talk, to eat solid food ...?

She only stopped talking when they came near to Kilfenora and David told them all to listen. They listened to the sound which was coming faintly over the hill; and then John Joe started to laugh.

'It's the Kilfenora Céilí Band,' he said. 'They must be practising. There's going to be a céilí on Saturday night.'

'Will you come with us, Bridget?' asked Mrs Arkins. 'Your poor mam won't be up to dancing, and your da is away, so come with us. You'll be very welcome.'

'So long as she doesn't expect me to dance with

her,' said John Joe. 'She's a bit heavy when she lands on your toes all the time.'

Mrs Arkins made a swipe at John Joe, but Bridget only laughed. She was in a really good mood; she felt that nothing could make her lose her temper.

They went on up the hill in silence, listening to the gay, jigging sounds of the dance music. But just as they reached the top of the hill and started down towards Kilfenora, the music suddenly stopped, and new sounds began — sounds which were sickeningly familiar to everyone in the summer of 1921. They were the sounds of a lorry revving, of wild, drunken voices, and of shots being fired. The Black and Tans had arrived.

By the time they reached the village, the lorry had stopped and the Black and Tans were pouring out of it, leaving just the driver and another man — a man with a coat over his head — sitting beside him. The lorry was parked in the middle of the street, where no one could get past it.

David spoke to the horse and guided him to the side of the road, well away from the lorry. Bridget clenched her hands and moved closer to Mrs Arkins. Everyone else sat silently and waited.

The Black and Tans were running up and down the street, hammering on doors. Bridget couldn't hear what they were saying until one of them crossed the street and banged on the door of a house nearby. Then she heard, and suddenly her face felt cold and damp, as if a sudden mist had hit her.

What the Black and Tan had said was, 'Do you know a man called Mike McMahon?'

The woman shook her head and closed the door, but for a moment her eyes met Bridget's. The warning in them was so unmistakable that Bridget wouldn't have been surprised if the Black and Tan had immediately come over to the cart and begun to question her.

He didn't, however. All the Black and Tans' attention was centred on the house where the céilí band had been practising. There was a lot of angry shouting; and then all the precious musical instruments, which had taken so long to save up for, were thrown out onto the road. The lorry deliberately reversed over them, smashing every one. The members of the céilí band were sent on their way at gunpoint.

And then the moment that Bridget had been dreading arrived. One of the Black and Tans came over to the cart and said to David Arkins, 'Do you know a man called Mike McMahon?'

There was a moment's silence. Bridget's heart was pounding so heavily that she was sure the Black and Tan would hear it.

Just when she felt that she could bear the tension no longer, David spoke, his voice polite and relaxed.

'Would that be Mike the Bridge, or Mike the Cashel, or Mike Aughty?' he enquired.

'Mike McMahon, you fool,' said the Black and Tan impatiently.

'Well, they're all McMahons,' explained David. 'There are a lot of McMahons around here. Or maybe it's Mike the Shop you're looking for; or, there again, it could be Mike Cork.'

The Black and Tan looked puzzled and went away to speak to his commanding officer.

'This man has red hair,' he said, when he returned.

'Ah,' said David. 'That sounds like Mike Cork. He lives out by Lickeen Lake. He's got red hair.'

'Tell me how to get to his place, then,' said the Black and Tan.

'I will, to be sure,' said David obligingly, 'but it won't do you much good. He's down in Cork at the moment, and has been for the last month. That's why we call him Mike Cork,' he added. 'His mother came from Cork, and when she died, God have mercy on her, she left him and his brother a great farm down there.'

'Oh, get on with you,' said the Black and Tan in disgust. 'Go on, clear out of here!'

Not daring to say that the lorry was in the way, David turned the horse and went back the way he had come.

'I'll go around by the back roads,' he said to his mother in a low voice. 'No sense in annoying them.'

When they had gone a little way, Bridget cautiously turned her head and looked over her shoulder. The Black and Tans had climbed back into the lorry, and it was following them down the road. Quickly David pulled the horse onto the grass verge.

As the lorry passed the Arkinses' cart, Bridget's heart started to pound again. The coat had slipped off the head of the man who was sitting beside the driver, and she could see his face. It was the man whom she and John Joe had seen in the Ennistymon barracks. It was Curtin, the spy.

Bridget didn't say another word until the Arkinses dropped her at her gate. John Joe helped her to take her bicycle off the cart. He looked at her white, worried face with understanding.

'Would you like me to come up with you?' he asked.

Bridget shook her head. The lump in her throat was too great for speech. In any case, she knew what had to be done, and only the McMahons could do it.

Chapter Eleven

Oddly enough, Bridget slept quite well that night. It was the rumbling of the heavy lorry coming up the avenue which woke her up.

She jumped out of bed and dressed herself with shaking hands. By the time she had climbed down the ladder from her room, the Black and Tans were already banging on the door with the butts of their rifles. Maggie came out of the east bedroom, her face white and her hands protectively clasped over her swollen stomach.

'Will I open the door, Mam?' whispered Bridget, her lips suddenly dry.

Her mother nodded, and Bridget opened the bolt which was so seldom fastened. She was glad that it was she, not her heavily pregnant mother, who was elbowed aside by the impatient soldiers.

'Where's your husband?' asked one of them. 'Where's Mike McMahon?'

'He's not here,' said Maggie in a trembling voice. 'He's not here. He's gone to help his cousin in Galway.'

'A likely story,' sneered the soldier. 'Stand back — the girl, too. Over there, by the wall.'

Bridget and her mother moved across the room to stand by the wall. Bridget glanced out of the window and saw several Black and Tans behind the house.

They were taking no chances. If Mike McMahon was in the house, there would be no escape for him. She heard the horse neighing and the pig squealing: they were searching the animals' cabins as well.

Two of the Black and Tans went into the east bedroom, and through the open door Bridget saw them throwing clothes from the press onto the floor. They struck the feather mattress with their rifles and then, in an orgy of destruction, slit it open with their bayonets. There were goose-feathers everywhere, all over the floor and floating in the air. They trampled Mike's best suit and Maggie's Sunday dress. Bridget hoped desperately that they wouldn't find the gold necklace.

She decided to try a diversion. Deliberately she moved nearer to the ladder, casting anxious glances up towards the loft. The Black and Tans' officer noticed her. Setting one man to guard the door, he summoned the others, and they all went up the ladder. At the last moment, the officer grabbed Bridget by the arm and dragged her up the ladder too.

'Now let's see where your daddy's hiding,' he snapped, at the top. Without warning, he twisted Bridget's wrist viciously. The pain made tears spring to her eyes, but she shut her mouth tightly, determined that nothing he could do would make her cry out.

Luckily, one of the other Black and Tans had some decency. He said impatiently, 'Oh, leave her alone. It's easier to search. There isn't anywhere to hide, really, is there?'

He was right: it was a very poor place to hide in. There was Bridget's bed — a feather mattress on top of an old iron bedstead — which was soon slit open; there were a few of her clothes, hanging on nails from the rafters — it was obvious that there was nothing behind them; there was an old table, with Bridget's school-books scattered untidily over it; and there was a big wooden chest. The Black and Tans gave a quick glance into the little space by the chimney, which had once been a secret room, and then turned and looked at the chest.

The chest was big enough to hold a man. It had been in Bridget's family for a long time; her father had told her that it might be over three hundred years old. It hurt her almost as much as her twisted wrist to watch the way they hammered it with their rifle-butts, then thrust their bayonets into the splintered wood and wrenched the lid off its hinges. Once it was open, however, they turned away from it in disgust: it held nothing but Bridget's old clothes and a few toys.

The men clattered down the ladder again and Bridget followed slowly, feeling sick with pain, but determined to hide her wrist from her mother. The Black and Tans were busy in the outside cabins. The pig had been ejected from his piggery, and Bridget could hear the men swearing as they slipped and skidded in the filth. One of them had a pitchfork and was busy searching the manure pile. A large and evil-smelling lump hit the officer on the side of his face as he bent down to poke under a bush just outside the piggery. He swore fluently for about five minutes, and Bridget giggled to herself. She remembered the schoolmaster telling her that she had to improve her English vocabulary, and that she should try to learn ten new words a day during the holidays. Now she had at least twenty for him.

Her wrist was feeling better, and she was able to

enjoy the sight of the Black and Tans with their uniforms decorated with clots of pig manure. It'll take them a long time to get rid of that smell, she thought happily.

'What about the milking, Mam?' she asked in a whisper.

'Shh,' said Maggie warningly. 'Don't move, don't do anything to annoy them. They'll go soon if they find nothing.'

It doesn't look as if they're going to go too soon, though, thought Bridget. They seemed determined to find Mike McMahon; they must have had some definite information that he had been involved in the attempt on the West Clare Railway line.

The cows were beginning to drift up from the river meadows, where they usually spent the summer nights, and were obviously expecting to be milked. The officer looked at the animals and at their swollen udders.

'Who milks the cows, then, if your husband is really away?' he asked curtly.

'I do,' said Bridget, stepping forward bravely.

At that moment there was the rattle of rusty bicycle wheels on the avenue and John Joe arrived, his face yellowish under his tan and his dark eyes subdued and scared.

'Do you want a hand with the milking again, Bridget?' he asked.

Bridget could have hugged him.

'Yes, please,' she said, trying to sound normal. 'Da won't be back for at least another week, so if you don't mind helping me, that's great.'

'Let's get the buckets, then,' said John Joe, and they went into the house. John Joe's eyes flickered over the east bedroom and took in the mess on the floor, but he said nothing — just gave Bridget a puzzled look. In silence, they led the cows into the cow cabin and tied them to the iron hooks set in the wall; in silence they fetched the milking-stools and sat down, their foreheads pressed against the cows' warm flanks, hearing the shouts and curses of the Black and Tans over the familiar rhythmic ping of the milk squirting into the metal pails.

When the milking was finished, John Joe matter-of-factly harnessed the horse to the cart, placed the churn on the back and poured the pails of milk into it.

'Is it all right if I take the milk to the creamery now, sir?' he asked nervously, and received a nod from the officer in answer.

'*Sir!*' sneered Bridget; but she took care to keep her voice down to a murmur.

'Doesn't hurt,' replied John Joe equably. He's such a difficult person to annoy, thought Bridget.

'You go by yourself,' she said aloud. 'I'll stay with my mam.'

John Joe nodded and went off, driving the cart carefully down the steep avenue. Bridget remained standing outside the cottage, watching the Black and Tans. It looked as if they were giving up. A few of them had just come up from the river meadows, and the officer was looking at them sourly; it was obvious that they had found no sign of Mike McMahon.

Without a word, they climbed back into the lorry, turned around — knocking a lot of stones out of the garden wall — and drove down the avenue, leaving behind clouds of evil-smelling smoke.

Bridget and her mother looked at each other, hardly daring to hope.

'Will you tell him it's safe now, Bridget?' said Maggie.

'Let's wait a while. Let's wait until after John Joe comes back. He doesn't know about the souterrain. The fewer people who know about it, the better.'

When John Joe did come back, however, he had some rather worrying news.

'They've left a man, Bridget. He's hiding down the lane, in that big ash tree just below the shrine of Saint Brigid. You can't see him, but he'll have a good view of the farm. He'll see your da if he comes out from anywhere, and he'll see you if you take him food.'

'Well, let's give him something to keep him amused, then,' said Bridget. 'Mam, where's that basket? Put some bread in it, and a bottle of milk. We'll lead him away from the farm.'

Taking the basket, Bridget went around to the back of the house, closely followed by John Joe. When they reached the Togher Field, they looked around with exaggerated care, looking everywhere except into the big ash tree on the lane. Bridget was trying very hard not to giggle. She felt as if she were one of the players who sometimes put on shows in the village hall.

She made hand signals to John Joe and crept across the field, keeping in the shadow of the hedge. When they reached the lane, she stopped under the ash tree and spoke to John Joe.

'Oh, good, they've all gone,' she said, feeling a bit of a fool, but knowing that her father's life might depend on her ability to sound convincing. 'It's safe to bring him food now. Come on, John Joe.'

She crossed the lane, went into the Rough Field, neatly jumped the stream and crossed the High

Meadow. John Joe followed her, with a grin on his brown face that showed he was enjoying himself immensely.

Bridget's hearing was very good, and although the Black and Tan was obviously following with great care, she could distinctly hear him moving on the other side of the hedge. Without hesitation, she climbed the hill, going past the ancient stone cattle rings. She was going as fast as she could; the top of the hill was completely bare of trees and hedges, and she knew that the soldier wouldn't dare to follow them too closely there, so she was doing her best to increase the distance between them while she had the chance.

When they reached the top of the hill, she took the risk of glancing over her shoulder. There was no sign of the Black and Tan; he was probably hiding behind the stone walls of the cattle rings.

'Quick,' Bridget said, grabbing hold of John Joe's hand. They both ran helter-skelter down the hill to the stone quarry. It was a very old quarry, full of briars and blackthorn bushes; and, best of all, it had a little tunnel, hidden behind a clump of trees. The tunnel had been built a long time before, to provide a quick way to get cartloads of stone out onto the road. Bridget and John Joe had discovered it the summer before, during the school holidays, but they hadn't used it much. John Joe had been uneasy about it. 'That roof looks as if it's going to collapse any minute,' he had said. Even now, he hesitated before going in.

'Come on, this is an emergency,' muttered Bridget, and ran in. She heard John Joe's footsteps behind her — and then she caught him by the hand and crouched down behind a huge stone.

They could hear the Black and Tan clearly. He was

climbing down into the quarry, and his heavy boots had started a landslide of an unstable mound of shale gravel. They could hear him cursing. He didn't seem to be making any great effort to stay hidden. He must think we went the other way, thought Bridget.

John Joe cautiously crept to the edge of the tunnel. A few minutes later he was back.

'It's all right,' he said. 'I think he's gone the opposite way. He's probably going over towards that old empty house. He might think your da is there.'

Together they stood and listened. They could hear other voices now; obviously the lorry had been left parked nearby, and the other Black and Tans had joined in the search.

'Let's go out on the road,' said Bridget. 'We'll go in the opposite direction. We can go back to Drumshee around by Lough Fergus. I hope Mam has the sense to keep away from Da. It won't hurt him to stay in hiding for a day or two. He's nearly better now.'

'Where is he?' asked John Joe curiously. 'Where did you hide him?'

Bridget hesitated. She would have loved to tell him. After all, he had shared all her troubles during the past week.

She opened her mouth and then closed it again. She remembered the day, on her ninth birthday, when her father had told her the secret. He had made her promise faithfully, on the shrine of St Brigid, that she would never, ever, tell anyone outside the McMahon family about the souterrain.

'It's the secret of Drumshee,' he had said solemnly. 'It's always been kept a secret, and it must always stay a secret.'

'I'm sorry,' she said miserably. 'I really can't tell

you. I promised. I'm really sorry, John Joe. It's not that I don't trust you.'

'Oh, that's all right,' said John Joe easily. 'It's just as well that I don't know, really. What I don't know, I can't tell. You never know — the Black and Tans might get hold of me and ask me if I know where he is. Now I can say I don't, and it'll be the truth.'

'They might torture you,' said Bridget.

'Well, if they do, I'll give in immediately and tell them he's hiding out at Applevale House,' said John Joe with a satisfied air. 'They say it's a good idea to tell part of the truth when you're under torture. I read that in some book.'

'I can't see what good that —' Bridget began; and then she stopped, as they heard the familiar roar of a lorry. Quickly they dived into the hedge and held their breaths.

The lorry passed without hesitation and went thundering along the road towards Ennistymon. Bridget gave a sigh of relief.

'Well, that's them gone for the moment,' she said happily. 'But I'm going to tell Da to stay hidden for a few days. I'm sure they'll be back.'

'Well, don't tell me anything,' said John Joe nervously. 'I certainly don't want to be tortured. David was telling me that the Black and Tans tortured a man in Miltown Malbay. They kept cutting off bits of him until he gave in and told them everything he knew. Then they went and murdered all the men he had betrayed, and they killed him, too.'

What if they torture Da? thought Bridget, as she went up the avenue. He does know a secret. He has Michael Collins's list — the list that's dynamite for any man to keep ....

When she reached the top of the avenue, she climbed the steep bank and went into the fort. Carefully she looked around; then she lifted the flagstone and went down the steps.

Her father was asleep; she could hear him snoring. When she struck the flint to light the little candle, he woke instantly and looked at her in a startled way.

'Is everything all right?' he asked.

'Everything's fine,' said Bridget steadily. She hesitated. She knew what should be done, but it might be difficult to convince him.

'Da,' she said, 'do you remember the night when Michael Collins came to Drumshee?'

Mike gave a hasty glance around — almost as if he feared danger from that name, even here, in the depths of the earth.

'Yes,' he said.

'Well, I listened to you talking, and I know you're hiding something for Michael Collins.'

Mike's face flushed with anger. 'You shouldn't listen to what doesn't concern you,' he said shortly.

Bridget's face flushed too. It does concern me, she thought angrily. I'm the one who has to get you out of a mess when you get into one. Who rescued you from Applevale House?

She clenched her hands in order to stop herself speaking her thoughts aloud. It was no good making her father angry. She had to reason with him.

'John Joe was telling me about a man in Miltown Malbay,' she said slowly. 'The Black and Tans tortured him until eventually he gave in and told them all his secrets .... And then the Black and Tans went out and murdered all the men whose names he gave them.'

Mike's face darkened. He knows the story, Bridget

thought; he knows it's true. She could tell by looking at him. She had been wondering whether John Joe had just made up the story, but now she knew that it had really happened.

She stared at her father and forced herself to go on. At least she could take this one danger from him.

'Give me the list, Da,' she said. 'I know a secret hiding-place in Drumshee — not here, not in the souterrain. You don't know it, but the list will be safe there.'

She looked around the dimly lit room. From the corner of her eye, she saw her father's glance flicker over the far wall. That wall was different from the other three: they were made from squared-off blocks of limestone; this fourth wall was made from heavy, irregular boulders of the greenstone which had been used in the walls of the cottage and in all the field walls on the farm.

'It's over there, isn't it, Da? If they find you, they'll make you tell. But no one would ever think a child would know. Let me hide it, Da.'

He was wavering, Bridget knew. She could see the sweat breaking out on his forehead. He was still weak from the fever. I can boss him, I know, she thought exultantly.

'It's in that wall, isn't it?' she asked. 'You might as well tell me, or I'll find it myself. You won't be able to stop me.'

'There's a loose stone in the middle there,' said Mike reluctantly, his voice sounding hollow and exhausted. 'See that one there, with the sharp bits sticking out of it? Take it out carefully. Don't hurt yourself. Those stones are heavy.'

Carefully, Bridget lowered the stone to the ground.

Behind it was a hollow space, and in the space was a box — a lead-grey box with a strange, interlacing pattern on its lid. Bridget carefully took it out.

'Where are you going to put it?' asked her father.

'What you don't know, you can't tell,' said Bridget pertly, and escaped up the stairs before he could question her any more.

Well, Michael Collins, she thought as she ran across the fort, I'm as good as your cousin now.

When she came to the edge of the fort, she looked around to make sure that no one was watching and then slipped under the tentlike branches of the ancient ash tree. There, in the quiet darkness, stood the little figure of St Brigid. It was a strange statue, shaped like a little old woman wrapped in a shawl, carved from a single big piece of stone.

Bridget knelt down, put aside the little bronze vase which was always kept filled with flowers, and lifted out the heavy stone statue. Under the statue was a flagstone; and only Bridget knew that under this was a small hollow space. She had discovered it a few years before, but she had never told anyone about her discovery, in case she was punished for playing with a holy statue.

The little lead box fitted the hollow as if it had been made for it. Bridget replaced the flagstone and the little statue, picked some fresh ferns and some pink ragged-robin flowers for the little vase, and then knelt down and joined her hands.

'Please, Saint Brigid, help Drumshee to keep Michael Collins's secret safe,' she prayed.

Chapter Twelve

For the rest of Friday evening, Bridget was kept busy helping her mother to tidy the cottage and stitch up the torn featherbeds. So it was later than usual when she rolled out of bed on Saturday morning. She could hear her mother, in the yard, talking to John Joe's brother David. She washed and dressed and went down to join them.

'John Joe's gone to Ennis with Mam,' David was saying, 'so I came down to give you a hand with the milking.'

'You're very good, all of you,' said Maggie.

A wave of shame came over Bridget. We shouldn't have to depend on neighbours all the time like this, she thought.

She had her breakfast, and then, when David had taken the milk to the creamery on his own cart, she filled a can with porridge and another with tea and climbed up to the fort. Everything was very quiet; there was no sound of lorries and no sign of anyone anywhere. Bridget lifted the flagstone and went carefully down the stone steps.

Mike was in good form.

'Is that all?' he said. 'I could eat an egg and a few rashers. I've been awake for ages, and I'm starving.'

'Well, that's all you're getting,' snapped Bridget.

She was out of patience with him this morning. Something about the way her mother had held her arms around her body the day before, protecting the unborn baby, had sickened her, and she felt very critical of Mike. It was a strange feeling for her; she had always adored her father, had always been sympathetic to his longing for freedom for Ireland, but now all she could think of was the trouble and the danger.

'You should leave politics to the young men without families, like Michael Collins told you to,' she said primly. 'Then you could be sitting in your own house and looking after your wife.'

Mike went red with anger, but after a moment he calmed down and looked at her thoughtfully.

'You know, Bridget,' he said, 'this room has probably seen a lot of our family's history. I was thinking about it when I was lying here this morning. My own father, Martin — Lord have mercy on him — told me that, when he was twelve years old, he slept here because his mother had the black fever. One night, while he and his sisters and brother were asleep, his mother died. His father buried her outside the fort, just near the shrine of Saint Brigid, and left a note on the kitchen table to say that he had the fever too; and then he walked away. They searched everywhere for him, but they never saw him again.'

'I know. You told me about that before.' Bridget was still impatient with him. The first time she had heard that story, she had cried for ages; it had seemed the saddest thing she could imagine. But now all she could think of was her mother and the new baby soon to be born.

'I think it was knowing what he suffered that got

109

me into politics in the first place,' Mike went on. 'My father had to scrimp and save for the rent all his life. I own the farm now; but I can never have any real security while England owns Ireland.'

'The Black and Tans made an awful mess, Da,' Bridget said, trying to make him understand what he was putting them through. 'They slit the beds with those sharp things on the ends of their guns, the walls are all dirty because they stuck sticks up the chimney and brought down all the soot — you remember Mam's been asking you to sweep the chimney for months — and they smashed that old chest in my room. Mam and I spent half the night trying to get everything straight.'

Her father shifted restlessly, a slight flush on his freckled face. 'Couldn't you get the Arkinses to help?' he asked guiltily.

'The Arkinses are doing everything for us,' snapped Bridget, picking up the empty cans. 'They haven't asked any questions, either, although they must be wondering how a man could leave his wife to manage on her own when she's expecting a baby in a few weeks' time.'

'Oh, for God's sake!' shouted Mike. 'Stop trying to torture me, Bridget! I've a lot on my mind!'

'And so have I a lot on my mind!' Bridget yelled back, her face scarlet with temper. 'And it's not fair, Da! You have a right to do what you like with your own life, but you've dragged Mam into it, and she never wanted anything to do with it in the first place. She just wants to lead a normal life with her husband and her children, and not have the Black and Tans coming in at all hours and turning the house upside down.'

Chapter Twelve

'A tidy house is not as important as the freedom of your country, Bridget,' Mike said — more quietly now, but Bridget could see him clenching his fists with the effort of controlling his temper. She didn't care. She was suddenly overwhelmed with sympathy for her mother.

'It's not just the things about the house that worry Mam!' she shouted. 'She's sick with nerves all the time from worrying about you. And what happens if you get taken off to prison — sent to England, or worse? The Black and Tans might shoot her, too, or burn the house — and even if they don't, Mam wouldn't be able to manage the farm without you. She'd starve. And then there's the baby — what would happen to the baby? And to me? Have you even *thought* about all this?'

Without another glance at her father, she climbed back up the steps, lifted the flagstone and, for the first time ever, went out without checking that there was no one around.

And then, suddenly, she felt as if her heart had stopped. From the yard came the sound of rough English voices and the stink of a lorry. Of course, from underground, she hadn't heard them coming.

As she stood there, wondering what to do, one of the soldiers looked up and caught the gleam of red hair in the fort.

'There's the girl, sir!' he shouted. They all came pouring up through the gap in the trees, climbing the steep slope to the fort.

Bridget had only seconds in which to act. If they caught her there, they would undoubtedly see the flagstone in the ground. Even if she ran away, they wouldn't bother to follow her. Why should they?

They had no interest in her. They only wanted to catch Mike McMahon.

There was only one thing which might stop them, and Bridget didn't hesitate. Bending down, she picked up a sod of earth and flung it as hard and as accurately as she could. It burst open right across the entrance of one of the beehives which faced the way in to the fort.

Bridget's father had told her that there are about forty thousand bees in a hive, and it looked as if every one of them came out, in an angry, buzzing black cloud, and made straight for the men who were pouring into the fort. If she had been less tense, Bridget would really have enjoyed the scene — the screams, the yells, the curses as the men turned and fled back towards their lorry.

Maggie had gone back into the cottage and closed the doors and windows. Bridget went and stood beside the duck pond, ready to plunge in if the swarm of bees showed any sign of coming towards her.

Then she heard the sergeant say, 'My God, Tommy's even got stings on his tongue. We'd better get him to a doctor, double quick. Get in the lorry, lads.'

'What about McMahon?' shouted one of the men, who seemed to have escaped the bees.

'He can wait,' the sergeant shouted back. 'We'll be back in a couple of hours. He can't get away; we have roadblocks everywhere. We'll get him, don't you worry about that.'

After the sound of the lorry had died away, Bridget went to the gate. The bees were still buzzing angrily in the fort, so she didn't want to go back that way. In any case, she wondered whether the Black and Tans might have left a spy watching the farm, just as they had before. Carefully, she looked into every tree, but there was no sign of anyone. Probably they had all been too frightened of the bees, and had driven off too quickly, to think up any plan like that.

'Have they gone?' asked Maggie in a frightened whisper, when Bridget arrived back at the cottage.

'Yes,' said Bridget. 'I threw a sod of earth at the hives and set the bees on them,' she added proudly. 'Did you see them?'

She giggled a little at the memory, and a smile came over Maggie's pale face.

'You're a rascal,' she said fondly. 'I never know what you'll be up to next. Well, let's hope that's the last we'll see of them for a while.'

'They said they'd come back in an hour or two,' said Bridget unhappily, hating to see the smile fade from her mother's face and the tight lines of worry come back to her mouth.

'Oh, well,' sighed Maggie. 'I suppose there's no point in sitting around and waiting for them to turn up. What do you think — shall we get the place ready for the new baby? It would take our minds off things a bit, wouldn't it?'

'Don't you think you'd better rest, Mam?'

'No,' said Maggie firmly. 'I'll feel better when I know everything is right. You get some lumps of lime out of the cabin and put them in the bucket with some water, and we'll limewash the walls.'

Bridget carefully poured water onto the lumps of lime and stirred the mixture with a stick until it was smooth and creamy.

'I'll do the tops of the walls, Mam,' she said. 'You do the lower bits, then you won't have to stretch.'

Together they whitewashed the walls of the

kitchen and of the bedroom. Then Bridget scrubbed the grey flagstones in the kitchen, and her mother sanded the big table under the window and black-leaded the range, until all the old familiar smells were overlaid with the sharp, clean, acrid odours of lime and soap.

'I'll wash the curtains, Bridget, if you'll clean —' Maggie began; but then they heard the familiar revving sound, and the stink of oil overwhelmed the smell of lime in the little kitchen. Bridget's heart sank. Won't we ever be free of the Black and Tans? she thought. But she faced the door bravely. It was worse for her mother than for her, she knew that.

The sergeant was in a towering rage. Bridget knew that straight away. He had been stung pretty badly; there was a big swelling on his neck, just above the collar of his black jacket, and one eye was almost closed by another sting.

'We've had enough of this nonsense,' he said roughly, as he came in the door. 'One of my men tells me that this girl threw a sod of earth at the beehive and caused the bees to attack us. I'm taking her down to Ennistymon with me. She'll spend the night in the barracks, and then it'll be off to Ennis Jail with her.'

'You can't do that!' cried Maggie, putting her arm around Bridget and pulling her close to her swollen body. 'You can't do that. She's only a child.'

'She's old enough to cause a lot of harm,' said the sergeant coldly. 'One of my men is in hospital after her bit of fun.'

He looked at Maggie's frantic face, at the tears beginning to pour down it. He seemed more interested in her than in Bridget.

'Unless, of course,' he added slowly, 'you were able

to tell me where your husband is. If you did that for me, I might be able to forget this piece of nonsense. After all, as you say, she's only a child.'

Maggie stiffened. Bridget tore herself free and faced the sergeant, her cheeks blazing with rage.

'She's told you again and again that my father's in Galway!' she said furiously, praying that her mother would realise that the Black and Tans couldn't do much to her, but that they would certainly put Mike McMahon in prison for years, or worse.

'Why don't you go away and leave us in peace?' she added, feeling that she would love to kick the sergeant in the shins.

His only answer was to grab her firmly by the arm and drag her towards the door. He wasn't looking where he was going, however, because his eyes were on Maggie; so he almost cannoned into a burly man, dressed in clerical black, who stood squarely in the little doorway.

'Well, good evening, everybody,' said the priest's gentle voice, just as Maggie was saying, 'Stop — I'll ....'

'Good evening, Father,' said Bridget breathlessly. She had never been so pleased to see Father Kiely in her life. He was a kind, gentle, patient man, but he could be a holy terror towards anyone who was cruel to a child or an animal. Maybe he'll be able to help us, Bridget thought.

'How are you all?' he asked, looking vaguely around the little room, not seeming at all surprised by the Black and Tans' presence.

'We're in a bit of trouble, Father,' said Maggie, with a gasp of relief. 'These soldiers want to take Bridget away with them, and her father is in Galway.'

Father Kiely smiled. 'And what's the bold, bad

Bridget been doing now?' he asked with amusement.

'It's no joke,' said the sergeant shortly. 'This girl set the bees on me and my men. One of them is in hospital at the moment.'

'I suppose they were swarming, Bridget, were they?' enquired Father Kiely.

'Yes, Father,' said Bridget, wondering what sort of sin it was to tell a lie to a priest.

'Very late year for swarms,' said Father Kiely, turning to the sergeant. 'I hope you've managed to get something for those stings. They're nasty, bee stings. You have to take care of them.'

'Come on,' said the sergeant brusquely, starting to pull Bridget towards the door again. 'We must be on our way.'

Maggie gave a little cry, but the square form of the priest didn't move from the doorway.

'I don't think you can do that, you know,' he said quietly. 'She's much too young. You're only nine, aren't you, Bridget?'

'Yes, Father,' replied Bridget. This time there was no hesitation in her voice. Well, if he can tell a lie, I can, she thought defiantly. A slight worry crossed her mind. Perhaps he really had forgotten her age .... But she put the thought out of her mind. She had always been told that it was rude to argue with anyone older than herself.

'So you see,' continued Father Kiely, 'she's much too young for you to take away.'

'I can't help that,' said the sergeant obstinately. 'I'm taking her. She's old enough to know what she was doing.'

'Well, in that case, I had better come too and talk to your commanding officer,' said the priest pleasantly.

After a minute, the sergeant dropped Bridget's arm.

'As she's only a child,' he said, 'we'll let her off this time. But her father's old enough to answer for what he does, and when we get our hands on him — and we will — he'll be coming away with us for a long, long time.'

He signalled to his men with a jerk of the head, and they all trooped out.

Bridget held her breath. A minute later she heard the lorry skidding down the avenue, and she let out a great sigh of relief.

'Well, so they're gone,' said Father Kiely placidly. 'Perhaps you could make your mother and me a nice cup of tea, Bridget.'

Chapter Thirteen

Sunday 10 July 1921

On Sunday morning, Maggie didn't feel well enough to go to mass. She had a pain in her back and said she ached all over. Bridget gave her a cup of tea in bed and then brought Mike his porridge.

The church bells had finished ringing by the time Bridget reached the gate at the end of the avenue, but it was downhill all the way to the church, and the priest was only just starting to say the opening prayer as she came in.

She knelt at the back, but John Joe had seen her come in, and he raised his eyebrows enquiringly. She nodded and smiled, and he looked reassured.

Was it really only a week ago, Bridget thought wonderingly, that I knelt in this church, not knowing where Da was or what had become of him? Now she knew where he was, but he wasn't safe yet. If we ever get him out of this mess, she promised herself, I'll never speak to him again if he doesn't get out of the IRA.

Outside the church, it was warm and sunny. The people, dressed in their Sunday best, stood around for a long time, chatting to one another and exchanging news of the week that had gone by. Everyone wanted to know how Bridget's mother was and whether Mike had come home yet. A few glances were exchanged when Bridget said, 'No, not yet.' She moved hurriedly over to where John Joe was standing.

'Shh,' he said, looking at some men who were leaning against the wall. 'Shh, I'm trying to listen.'

Bridget listened too, and her heart filled with excitement. The men were talking about Ennistymon and the Black and Tans.

'Loads and loads of them were getting on the train to Ennis last night,' said one man.

'Yes, and I saw two lorries going off at about the same time,' said another. 'And you should have seen the cut of one of them getting into the lorry. He had the face swollen out on him. I don't know what had happened to him at all. He looked like he'd been in a prizefight.'

Bridget could hardly stop laughing. They drew away from the men, and as she pushed her bicycle up the road beside John Joe she told him what had happened the day before — how the bees had come raging out of the hive and stung the Black and Tans, how they had tried to drag her off to prison, and how Father Kiely had saved her.

'Well, if there's some big operation in Ennis, that should keep them out of the way for a few days. Do you think they'll be back?'

'Sure to be,' said Bridget pessimistically.

'And what'll you do then?'

'Oh, I don't know. I'm sick of worrying about it. Let's go home.'

At that moment, John Joe's brother David called out, 'I'm off to do our milking, Bridget, so if you and John Joe do yours, I'll come and collect the churn and take it down to the creamery with ours.'

'Right,' said Bridget, getting on her bicycle. 'I'll

get the pails out and have everything ready by the time you arrive.'

'I'll be there before you,' boasted John Joe, and he set off running as fast as he could. Bridget overtook him, but she was slowed down by having to open the gates and to push her bicycle up the steep avenue; so they arrived at the house, breathless and laughing, at the same moment.

Maggie was out of bed and dressed, but she looked very pale and she complained of backache. She shouldn't have done all that cleaning and painting yesterday, thought Bridget, looking at her in a worried way.

'Parents are such a worry, aren't they?' she said to John Joe, as they went out to do the milking.

'Are they?' said John Joe in astonished tones. 'I never really think about mine at all, and I certainly don't worry about them.'

'Well, you're lucky, then. I wish I were the youngest in a big family. I bet David worries about your mam and da.'

'The only things David worries about are girls and getting out in time for dances,' said John Joe light-heartedly. 'Don't you worry, now. It'll all work out all right.'

Bridget hoped he was right, but she doubted it. The Black and Tans had her father's name, and they knew where he lived; they would come back again and again until they found him.

However, if they had all gone away for the weekend, then Sunday just might be a peaceful day. Bridget decided to put the whole business out of her mind. It wasn't fair to John Joe for her to be so depressed all the time she was with him.

'I'm going to the creamery with John Joe and David, Mam,' she called in through the cottage window. 'I won't be long. Why don't you have a rest? I'll get the dinner when I come back.'

They had fun at the creamery. All the young people had the job of bringing the milk there on Sunday mornings, and quite a few of Bridget and John Joe's friends from school were already there. They all had a great time, laughing and kidding around, so it was nearly one o'clock when Bridget got back to the cottage.

There was no sign of her mother anywhere, and the hens were busily scratching in her precious flower-beds under the windows. Mam must be asleep, thought Bridget. By the look of those flowers, the hens must have been there for at least ten minutes, and normally they'd have been chased away the minute they came around to the front of the house.

She went into the cottage, and her heart sank as she heard a groan from her mother's room.

'It's not fair,' she muttered rebelliously under her breath. 'I can never have any fun. There's always something.'

She went into the bedroom and looked impatiently at her mother. Maggie wasn't in bed, as Bridget had expected her to be; she was standing at the window, hunched in pain, with her hand pressed to the small of her back.

'Oh, Bridget, thank God you've come at last. I'm getting terrible pains. Help me into bed and go and get Mrs Arkins. I think the baby is coming early. Get down those clean sheets from the press and make up the bed first, though.'

'Mam, I'll get Mrs Arkins first. Sure, she won't care

if there are clean sheets or not. She's not like that.'

'Do as I tell you, Bridget,' said Maggie, tightening her lips as another wave of pain hit her. 'Oh, and bring me a cloth — there's a smear on this window. And put the darning away in the press ....'

'Lord, give me patience,' prayed Bridget; but then, suddenly, she remembered that Mrs Arkins had told her that a woman always wants to get everything perfect just before a baby arrives.

I suppose the best thing to do is just to humour her, she thought, as she ran here and there. It was another quarter of an hour before she got her mother into bed, and then a terrible wave of pain left Maggie exhausted and gasping.

'I'm going for Mrs Arkins,' said Bridget resolutely. 'Stop fussing, Mam. Everything looks fine.'

At that moment another pain hit Maggie, and she gave an agonised scream which terrified Bridget. She clung to Bridget's hand, and little drops of sweat ran down her face. She was gripping so tightly that Bridget felt her hand go numb.

'Don't leave me,' she gasped. 'Stay with me, Bridget.'

Bridget stayed, but she didn't know what to do. She was terrified that the baby would actually be born and she wouldn't be able to help in any way. She had never even been in a house where a baby was being born. She had a vague idea that she should be boiling pots of water, but her mother wouldn't let go of her hand.

The hours went on and the sun moved around in the sky towards the west, but still the pains came every few minutes, with clockwork regularity. Maggie hardly seemed conscious, and Bridget knew that this was no ordinary birth. She had to do something, but she didn't dare leave her mother for long enough to go right down to the Arkinses' house. In any case, Mrs Arkins might not even be in; Sunday afternoon was a great time for visiting friends and neighbours.

No, there was only one thing to do. Bridget gently took her hand out of her mother's limp one and ran out of the cottage, up to the fort.

'Da!' she said urgently, as she ran down the stone steps of the souterrain. 'Da, you must come. It's Mam. The baby's coming, and she's awful bad. I don't know what to do.'

It was a bit of a struggle getting Mike up the steps and then down the slope and into the house, but they managed. The relief of having someone to share the responsibility with made Bridget feel almost light-hearted. But when Mike saw the state his wife was in, he was aghast.

'You'll have to go for the doctor, Bridget,' he said. 'Get on your bicycle, like a good girl, and cycle into Kilfenora. Tell him to come straight away.'

'Oh, Da, I can't do that! He might give you away to the Black and Tans,' said Bridget in alarm.

'Never mind about that,' said her father roughly. 'Better for me to be in prison than for your mam to die here in her own bedroom. Do what I tell you and go as quickly as you can. Don't worry; Dr Carrigg is a good man, not like that fellow in Corofin. He'll come, and he'll mind his own business about me.'

Bridget got her bicycle and rode down the steep hill of the avenue so fast that, when she reached the gate, she couldn't stop; she had to throw herself off the bicycle and into the bank behind the gate piers. Shaken and bruised, she picked herself up and, leaving the gate open for once, cycled as fast she could down the road towards Kilfenora.

Afterwards she could never remember that journey. It was as if her mind, unable to take any more worry, simply shut down. She cycled mechanically until she reached Kilfenora and was hammering on Dr Carrigg's door.

What will I do if he's not there? she thought despairingly; but the door opened, and the doctor himself stood there.

My father was right, thought Bridget: Dr Carrigg is a good man. He listened quietly to what Bridget had to say; then he got his medical bag and opened it. Bridget thought that perhaps he was going to give her some medicine for her mother, but he took out a sweet and gave it to her.

'You're a brave girl, Bridget,' he said, very kindly. 'Now, you leave your bicycle there at the back of the house, and you can have a ride back with me in my car. Don't worry. I'll see to your mother.'

At any other time, Bridget would have really enjoyed her first ride in a car, and the thought of telling John Joe all about it; but she was so worried about her mother that she was just relieved they were going so fast. They swept through the open gate and up the avenue, scattering the hens, who ran squawking for cover in the orchard. Dr Carrigg jumped out of the car, leaving the door open, and ran into the cottage.

As soon as he got into the bedroom, however, he was calm and reassuring.

'Now, Mrs McMahon, you're going to be fine. Just don't you worry about anything. Bridget, why don't you take your father out to the kitchen? You can be making us all a cup of tea. Put on a good big kettle, like a good girl. I'll need lots of hot water in a while.'

Bridget made a pot of tea, but the doctor was busy and her father had no heart for it, so she ended up throwing most of it away. The big kettle of water hanging from the iron crane boiled and boiled, and Bridget topped it up three or four times, but still Dr Carrigg stayed in the bedroom, and still Maggie's cries of agony went on.

It was a relief to Bridget when the clock struck six and John Joe and David arrived to help with the milking. David was very nice; he told Bridget stories about the day John Joe had been born, and about what a funny little red-faced object he had been.

'Your mam won't even remember all the pain, once the baby's born,' he said. 'She'll be in great form then. When I get back from the creamery I'll send our mam up and she'll help with the baby.'

After they had gone, Bridget went back into the kitchen, feeling quite a bit better. She sat down beside her father, and saw him lift his head and listen.

The cries of pain suddenly stopped, but another sound replaced them, and Bridget knew what it was. It was the sound of a baby crying.

The bedroom door opened, and Dr Carrigg came out with a bundle in his arms.

'Well, Mr McMahon,' he said, 'you've got a son — and, my God, he's a big bruiser of a fellow! He'll be out sowing potatoes in a year or two's time.'

Bridget thought she had never heard anything so funny. She laughed until tears ran down her face.

Her father went towards the bedroom door, but the doctor stopped him.

'Your wife's having a bit of a sleep,' he said. 'Give

her a while and she'll be fine. Sit and hold your son for a bit.'

'Give him to Bridget,' said Mike. 'She's been the one in charge of the family for the last ten days.'

'What are we going to call him, Da?' asked Bridget, uncovering the little face.

'Well, I was thinking about calling him Martin, after my father. He was a fine man, God have mercy on him.'

'Why not let him have a name for himself?' said Bridget, suddenly feeling impatient with all this dwelling on the past. 'Your father had a sad life. We want this little fellow to have a happy one.'

'Well, you think of a name for him, then,' said Mike meekly. 'What will we call him?'

'I'd like to call him James,' said Bridget decisively. 'I read a book about a boy called James, a while ago, and I think it's a really nice name.'

'Well, James it is, then, if your mother agrees,' said Mike, placing a chair for Dr Carrigg.

The doctor sat down by the fire and took his pipe out of his pocket. He smoked quietly for a few minutes, while Bridget nursed the baby and kissed his perfect little fingers. She almost felt like crying, either from joy or from relief — she didn't know which.

But when Dr Carrigg spoke, she stiffened with apprehension.

'I hear you've been away for a while,' he said, looking straight at Mike.

'Yes, I have,' Mike replied, looking steadily back at the doctor.

'Well, keep it to yourself for today, but tomorrow there's going to be a ceasefire, a truce, declared for

both sides. All the boys will be let out of prison, and while the truce lasts there will be no more fighting. Let's hope it does last — that the fighting doesn't start again for any reason.'

Mike drew in a deep breath. 'Well, I can tell you one thing, Doctor,' he said quietly. 'If it does start again, there's one man here who'll have no part in it.'

Bridget lifted the baby up in her arms and kissed his soft little cheek.

'Do you hear that, James McMahon?' she said. 'You're going to have a bit of peace around you while you're growing up. I could do with some peace myself. I don't think I could stand another fortnight like this one.'

～

A few weeks later, Michael Collins visited Drumshee again. The night before he arrived, Bridget took the little box from its secret hiding-place and gave it to her father.

By the time she got up the next morning, Michael Collins had already left. Bridget was glad she hadn't seen him. It had hurt her to see the look of shame on her father's face over the past few weeks. But now, she was relieved to see, he looked like his old self again, and he acted like someone who has had a great load taken off his shoulders.

Bridget didn't ask her father what Michael Collins had said to him. Those two weeks of midsummer were beginning to fade from her mind, and she never wanted to think of them again. She just wanted to live in peace at Drumshee, with her father and her mother and her new baby brother, little James.

And, for six months, there was peace. Then the fighting broke out again; but this time it was between Irishmen — between those who, like Michael Collins, wanted peace and a treaty with England, even at the cost of a divided country, and those who, like Eamon De Valera, rejected the Treaty and wanted to fight on.

But Mike McMahon kept his word and didn't join in. So there was still peace at Drumshee — peace for James to grow into a sturdy little boy, and for Bridget to finish her schooling.

And then it would be time for her to spread her wings and join her cousin Kitty, and her best friend John Joe, out in America.